# NEEDLE IN A HAYSTACK

*Sixth in the Series of Stories About Growing Up
in and Around Small Towns in the Midwest*

**Edited by
Jean Tennant**

Shapato Publishing, LLC
Everly, Iowa

Published by:    Shapato Publishing, LLC
                 PO Box 476
                 Everly, Iowa 51338

ISBN: 978-0615919430
Library of Congress Control Number: 2012921097

First Printing September 2013

Interior artwork by LaVonne M. Hansen and Wesley Peters.

Thank you to Alvena Koehnk for the use of her photo
for the cover.

Sketch by LaVonne M. Hansen

# TABLE OF CONTENTS

# NEEDLE IN A HAYSTACK

*Sixth in the Series of Stories About Growing Up in and Around Small Towns in the Midwest*

Sketch by Wesley Peters

# PLAYING IN THE HAYLOFT

## Butch Weatherby

First of all, we weren't even supposed to be doing it. My sisters and I were given pretty much free reign to do what we wanted—within reason—around the farm, once our chores were done. And we spent a lot of time in the barn because of the families of cats there. But we'd been told to *not* climb up into the hayloft.

The barn was massive, and even back then it was old, with gaps between the boards that let in angled bands of light. There was a rickety wooden ladder leading up to and attached to the loft, which was probably about twenty feet above the barn floor. To us, however, the loft seemed a summit of immense height, and all the more tempting for that reason.

Sandwiched in between Carolyn, two years older, and Paulette, one year younger, I was always outnumbered, and never willing to back down from a challenge from my sisters. The first time we climbed the ladder into the hayloft the challenge came from Paulette. Ten years old at the time, Paulette was a tough little tomboy who wore dresses only to school and to church, and only then because she absolutely had to. Carolyn, just into her teens, was sweet and naturally feminine. She never would have been the first to suggest we defy our parents and climb the rickety ladder, but she was just as tempted by the forbidden fruit.

I went up first. Paulette wanted to, but a sense of brotherly protectiveness came over me and I insisted on testing the ladder's strength ahead of them. When I got to the top of the ladder I crawled belly-first onto the loft, then turned around and peered down at them.

Their upturned faces were small ovals far below, and I had to close my eyes for a couple of seconds to fight back a wave of vertigo.

They quickly grew impatient, hollering questions up at me. Was the ladder strong enough? Would the loft hold us all? Were there any kittens up there?

Yes, yes and no, I told them.

Paulette scrambled up next. Carolyn insisted, saying if Paulette fell she wanted to be below to catch her. The boards of the hayloft creaked and groaned beneath our weight, but when the three of us stood we felt as though we'd scaled Mount Everest. We moved cautiously at first. Even brave little Paulette was subdued and round-eyed with wonderment.

But there were wonders to behold, which soon caught our attention. Besides the loose hay that reached almost to the rafters, there were many old and rusting tools that we recognized, and a few we didn't. Pigeons cooed down at us, seeming unstartled by our presence. And far up in the deepest, darkest corners hung a few dark shapes that we hoped weren't bats.

There were also a few coils of thick rope. Best of all, one of the ropes was tied to an overhead rafter and dangled temptingly below. Of course Paulette was the first one to grab the rope and swing out into space, whooping loudly with glee. With her clinging to it, the rope arced around, then back, and Carolyn grabbed her around the waist and pulled her in.

We took turns swinging on the rope, heady with daring-do, terrified and thrilled at the same time.

Brave because our parents were gone for the day—Dad to a farm equipment auction with our uncle and Mom to visit her sister in the hospital—we swung and hooted with abandon, knowing this wouldn't last forever and determined to squeeze every bit of pleasure from the experience that we could.

On the floor of the barn was more loose hay, stored there until it would be needed, in piles ten to fifteen feet deep.

It didn't take long before we were tired of just swinging on the rope, and began letting go to fall into the mounds of hay. The next person with the rope always made sure the one before was out of the hay and the way was clear before going. But soon we were exhausting ourselves by swinging, dropping, and climbing the ladder for another turn, over and over.

It must have been after my fifth or sixth drop onto the hay that our fun came to an end. I'd landed on my back and lay there spread-eagle, laughing like crazy. But this time I didn't hear my sisters' encouraging calls for me to get out of the way, and I soon realized I was the only one laughing.

Lifting my head, I looked up into the rafters. Carolyn and Paulette were already climbing down the ladder. And they no longer looked like they were having fun. Far from it.

Crawling with some effort from the mound of hay, my feet hit the ground at about the same time they made it to the bottom of the ladder.

Mom, Dad and our Uncle Stan stood in the open doorway of the barn. They were all staring at us, and we had no idea how long they'd been there. Mom's expression was one of dismay. Dad looked angry, and Uncle Stan seemed to be amused.

Back then, parents usually held to the philosophy of "spare the rod and spoil the child." Though my sisters didn't get whipped, Carolyn was not allowed to attend a dance she'd been looking forward to and both girls were given extra chores for a month. I didn't get off so easy. I felt the sting of Dad's belt, though, looking back, I don't think he really put a lot of muscle into it. The message was the important thing, and he let me know I'd disappointed him.

A year or so later, a farm hand fell from the very hay loft where we'd been playing and broke his arm so badly that he never had full use of it again.

No one had to tell Carolyn, Paulette or me that there were good reasons behind our parents' rules.


**Harold "Butch" Weatherby** recently moved back to the farm place he grew up on in southern Iowa. With the help of some remodeling the house stands firm, but the old barn, alas, is no more.

Photo provided by Kent Stephens

# JAMES BOND 1967

## Kent Stephens

"Get your butt on that tractor seat and don't get off until I tell you," growled Uncle Melvin.

Only a few hours earlier I had been sitting in a nice comfortable seat on the California Zephyr train, enjoying the view of the countryside. My mother, sister and I arrived in south central Iowa from northern California that morning after a 48-hour journey. It was early June 1967. My mother and sister were going to visit family for a couple of weeks while I spent the summer working on the farm. I had spent every summer on one or another of the family farms since I was ten. Now, at seventeen, I would start my senior year of high school in September, making this my last full summer in Iowa, working on my Uncle Melvin's and Aunt Icie's farm.

Three tractors and plows were ready to go, one each for, Uncle Melvin, Ronald, my older cousin, and me. These were working tractors with no frills, no cabs, no air conditioning, no radios—not even an umbrella for shade. I was assigned the 450 Farmall with a four-bottom plow, the biggest and most powerful tractor they owned at the time. I didn't question the decision, and I loved running the 450 from the first time I climbed into it.

Just before sunrise, Ronald and I started our day. He checked the feed and water for the livestock while I fueled and greased the equipment. Then we headed back to the house for breakfast. The smell of breakfast cooking came from Aunt Icie's kitchen. Fresh eggs from her hens and bacon hot off the stove got us ready for a full day of work.

Quickly the days became routine. Up before sunrise, work until noon, return to the house for dinner, maybe a quick nap, then back to the field. Uncle Melvin would stop working in the field about 5:00 PM to do the evening chores. Around six he and Icie would come out to the field in the old pickup truck to bring a supper of the midday meal leftovers to Ronald and me. It was peaceful then, with the tractors shut off and the smell of warm, moist soil that had just been turned over. Supper on the tailgate was better than at any restaurant.

As a 4-H group leader Ronald had evening meetings to attend, but I would stay out until 10:00 PM before stopping. Everyone thought I was a little crazy for working into the night, but I didn't have anything special to do in the evenings so I figured I could get a little more work done. The darkness brought an entirely different perspective to the job. I had to be more aware of obstacles, but engines ran cooler and seemed more powerful after sunset. There was a feeling of isolation out in the fields, as I could see only as far as the work lights would shine.

The house had no shower, just a bathtub. I really preferred a shower and Ronald agreed with me, so we rigged up an outdoor shower made from a garden hose and a sprinkler head hung up in an oak tree between the house and the barn. The water for the shower came directly from the well, so it was cold. We convinced ourselves that hot showers were for sissies anyway, and after a long hot day on the tractor the cold water felt really good. Crude as it was, the shower was such a great treat for us that we didn't worry about privacy. If a car happened to pull up in the driveway, we would just hide behind the big oak until we got our clothes on.

At 10:00 PM the TV news came on from Des Moines, the most important segment was the weather. As Uncle Melvin, Ronald and I gathered around the TV, bowls of ice cream would magically appear, thanks to Aunt Icie. She would join us when *The Tonight Show* starring Johnny

Carson came on at 10:30. We'd watch the monologue and if the first guest was someone interesting, we stayed up a little longer. I don't think anyone ever made it to the second guest.

It seemed like we plowed forever. When the plowing was almost done, my uncle dropped out of the tractor work to concentrate on his other farm duties. Ronald and I started the disking, and when that was done Ronald would prepare the planter and fill it with seed. While he was doing that I switched over to harrowing to give the soil its final preparation before planting.

One Saturday afternoon Uncle Melvin came out to the field and grumbled to us, "Take the rest of the day off, but be back at work in the morning."

My butt had been on that tractor seat for twenty-seven straight long hot days. I was more than ready for a night in town.

We raced for the house, showered, slicked up and were ready for action, heading for Centerville. Even a flat tire on Ronald's car didn't slow us down. We changed that tire faster than any professional pit crew, being careful not to ruin our newly acquired good looks.

The theater was showing the new release of *You Only Live Twice*, starring Sean Connery as James Bond, the coolest guy in the world. With Cokes and a bucket of popcorn, we settled in to watch Mr. Bond save the world and kiss a few beautiful Bond girls in his spare time. It wasn't long before he spoke the famous signature line: "Bond, James Bond." We felt like we were right there with him, fighting the evil villain Ernst Blofeld. Busting up dirt clods in the corn field was far from our minds.

When the movie was over, Ronald and I *were* Bond. We swaggered out to our specially equipped Aston Martin DB5 (Ronald's Pontiac Catalina); we toured the cobbled streets of Monte Carlo (Centerville's bricked town square); and stopped at a local after-hours nightspot (Dairy Queen) for martinis, shaken, not stirred (hot fudge sundaes). Though we searched for Bond Beauties, we struck out. We weren't worried. We knew the Aston Martin would get us across the border into France in less than thirty minutes and on to new adventures (we went back to the farm).

Saving the free world is a lot of work. We slept in until an outrageous seven o'clock on Sunday morning before getting up and back to work.

Later that summer we made it to the county and state fairs. Uncle Melvin teased us, calling us slackers for taking so much time off when there was work to be done.

Even when the planting was finally done, it didn't mean the end of my job. I worked a rotary hoe on areas that had been planted and there was always cultivating to be done. I mowed, raked, baled and picked up hay along with the other basic farm chores.

Summer seemed to end entirely too quickly, and it was time for me to head back to California. Football practice started two weeks before school and I couldn't miss the first day of practice. So one evening I was off to catch the westbound California Zephyr, and two days later I was home. August football practice was actually easier than farm work in the hot and humid Iowa summer.

We had used more than 4,500 gallons of gas that season, getting the crop in. I was paid $8.00 per day plus room and board for full work days. Slacker days didn't count. I went home with a great suntan, stronger muscles, a huge sense of accomplishment, pride for a job well done and $248 in my pocket.

It was the best summer ever.


**Kent Stephens** was born and raised in Northern California, but spent most of every summer of his youth working on family farms around Osceola and Centerville, Iowa. Now retired from a diverse career in transportation, he lives with his wife, Kimberly, in Reno, Nevada. He spends his free time archiving family stories, photos and movies to DVDs for the rest of his family.

Sketch by LaVonne M. Hansen

Photo provided by Betty Hembd Taylor

# COUNT YOUR BLESSINGS

## Betty Hembd Taylor

On cold winter mornings, I woke to the sound of my father shaking ashes from the grates in the heater so he could lay a new fire. If he'd banked the coals just right the night before, some of the embers might still be glowing.

In the upstairs bedroom I shared with my sisters, I kept warm in my flannel pajamas under a pile of quilts. I couldn't see what Dad was doing, but I'd watched him lay a fire many times and I could visualize it all. It was reassuring to know he was making the house warm and comfortable for us, but reassurance was often accompanied by foreboding in my preschool days.

As a family, we sat down together for three meals a day and were expected to eat whatever was on the menu. Mom was a good cook, so that was not usually an issue. I liked some things better than others, but there was one thing I never learned to like or even tolerate. Oatmeal.

Dad scooped a generous supply of cobs from a box next to the stove, put them in the heater, tossed in a bit of kerosene, and lit them with a farmer's match. When the cobs were burning well, he laid kindling and coal over them and closed the iron door.

A stovepipe attached to the heater ran through a grate in the ceiling into our bedroom and connected to a chimney hole just above the closet. Before long, heat radiated from the stovepipe and warmed the room.

Soon I heard footsteps in the kitchen where Dad was going through the same process to start the kitchen range. When the fire was going well, he filled the tea kettle from the water bucket and set it on the stove.

Opening the stair door, he called to my brothers, "Roll out! Chore time!"

Having done what he could to make the house comfortable, he headed out to do the chores. Soon my brothers stumbled out behind him.

Before long I heard Mom in the kitchen, preparing cereal and coffee from hot water in the tea kettle. Health issues, a large family, and the Great Depression had taken a toll on my mother. She often comforted herself by singing hymns. On the morning that changed my life, she seemed to be hooked on "Count Your Blessings."

She opened the stair door and called to my sisters and me, "Time to get up." As she headed back to the kitchen, I could hear her singing, "So amid the conflict whether great or small, do not be discouraged; God is over all."

I thought about my own conflict with oatmeal but decided it was too late to pray for pancakes as breakfast was already on the stove. Maybe if I was lucky, we'd have Cream of Wheat or Malt-O-Meal. We dressed, went downstairs, and washed up in a basin on the washstand.

When the guys came in from doing the morning chores, they too washed up, and we all sat down to eat. As we bowed our heads, Dad blessed the food with the same prayer he used three times a day: "Lord God Heavenly Father, bless us and these thy gifts which we receive from thy bountiful goodness—through Jesus Christ our Lord. Amen"

Having noticed that the bountiful goodness we were blessed with was the dreaded oatmeal, I steeled myself for the worst.

Mom was something of an expert on nutrition. She studied bulletins from the County Extension Office and read the women's sections of farm magazines.

Research backed up her certainty that cooked oatmeal was the best breakfast for her healthy brood. Depending on what she had in the pantry, she did her best to dress it up a bit. We could choose to add cinnamon, raisins, white or brown sugar, fresh milk; and on rare occasions, nuts and coconut. But it wasn't the taste that did me in; it was the texture that seemed destined to hit my gag reflexes.

Mom set my portion before me, served in our favorite blue cereal bowl with Shirley Temple's picture on the bottom. "Eat your oatmeal," she said pleasantly. "It's good for you and will stick to your ribs 'til lunch time." Hoping to make it more palatable, she added some raisins and brown sugar.

I was certain my ribs would be just fine until noon. Everyone else was eating the healthful meal while I stirred mine with a spoon, took a few cautious bites—and gagged.

Dad looked at me sternly. "Don't play with your food."

I looked around hoping to see a glimmer of sympathy from the siblings, but saw none. They didn't seem to mind their oatmeal and were probably thinking about school and other things that did not include me. Perhaps they were annoyed that I was the one who had the Shirley Temple bowl as well as most of the attention.

Mom seemed to understand that the texture of the oatmeal bothered me, so she crumbled a few soda crackers on top to change it a bit; then doggedly encouraged me. "When you eat it all up you'll see Shirley Temple's face."

I ate the crackers and the raisins, took another bite, gagged again—then defiantly used my spoon to move the remainder of the mess to one side. "There she is!"

At that, the loving father, who had risen early to warm the house, lost his patience. "There are starving children in the world who would be happy to have a breakfast like that. Now, finish your oatmeal, and no more gagging."

I would have been happy to give the starving children my oatmeal but decided not to mention it. Dad looked stern so I weighed in. He shook his head but said no more in spite of another gag or two.

According to Newton's law of gravity, "What goes up must come down." Well, that morning what went down came back up. I threw up my oatmeal on the table. If my siblings had felt any sympathy for me in the first place, they'd have quickly lost it along with their appetites.

The day that began with apprehension, escalated to disaster, but in the days that followed, I learned it had culminated in a miracle. No one ever again demanded or even encouraged me to eat oatmeal.

As my grandmother used to say, "God works in mysterious ways."

Before long, I was surprised and thankful to see a brand-new product called Cheerioats (later renamed Cheerios) on our breakfast table. Mom was quite certain it wasn't as good for me as cooked cereal and would not stick to my ribs as well. Still, unlike Wheaties and Post Toasties, it was made from oats—and that was indeed a blessing. As I helped Mom clear the breakfast table she was singing again.

> "When upon life's billows you are tempest tossed
> When you are discouraged thinking all is lost
> Count your many blessings, name them one by one
> And it will surprise you what the Lord has done."

**Betty Hembd Taylor** of Hartley, Iowa, holds true to some traditions from her past. She has frequently annoyed her children and grandchildren by off-key singing while working about the house. Unable to tolerate statins or traditional oatmeal made from rolled oats, she keeps her cholesterol under control by preparing oat bran, steel cut oatmeal, and oat bran muffins.

# SPAM SANDWICHES

## Patrick Hoffman

While my father was gone for more than two years during World War II, our family, like so many others, went through a period where rationing was the norm and a dollar had to be stretched until it wept.

Our mother became an expert at budgeting. Instead of buying new, she mended the clothes my younger brother Steve and I wore. Using scraps of fabric left over from other projects, she would add length to our pants as our legs grew. Though she did her best to match the fabric, we sometimes walked around looking like refugees from clown camp.

Steve got my hand-me-downs, most of which had already been patched three times over, while I was the recipient of our cousin Herman's outgrown clothes. Herman was an only child, and doted on by his parents. He was also something of a dandy. When the twice-yearly box arrived from Aunt Florence, our mother would sort through the hodgepodge of knit sweaters, linen shirts and short pants. I'd watch and hope for a pair of dungarees. Sometimes it happened. Once there was a black wool sailor-style shirt and pants I liked, but it arrived in July and the summer sun beat down on me in the outfit. I began to sweat, which made the wool itch, which made me scratch and sweat even more until I was forced to flee inside, stripping off pieces of clothing as I ran.

Steve laughed at that, getting his revenge because he had liked the sailor outfit too and had been disappointed that I'd gotten it.

We made other concessions to a tight budget. All families were issued ration books, greatly limiting the amount of sugar and meat each could buy. Mom adjusted her recipes to use what we had. She made sugarless cake, using corn syrup to sweeten it, and her cookies with molasses were nearly as good. We had a Victory Garden in our back yard, which Mom planted and Steve and I weeded every day.

We also had a few chickens in the back yard, to provide us with eggs, and Mom warned us not to befriend them. A clucking, two-legged pet one day might very well be supper the next. And without a car, we didn't worry about the gas rationing.

There was one thing, however, of which there never seemed to be a shortage. Spam. The unmistakable rectangle shape made an appearance at our table at least twice a day, and more often three. Most mornings it rested next to the eggs on our plates. The mothers in our neighborhood shared recipes, and as a result Spam was sliced, diced, cubed, and ground; mixed with rice, folded into macaroni and cheese, layered on biscuits and covered with gravy.

Mom, through creative experimentation of her own, seemed to have an endless number of ways to get us to eat Spam. "It's good for you," she insisted, setting our plates in front of us. "And growing boys need plenty of meat."

With one elbow on the table, I used my fork to push the food around on my plate. A year earlier I'd actually liked Spam, but over the ensuing months my enthusiasm for it had waned. "What's Spam mean, anyway?" I asked, regarding it with suspicion.

Mom admitted she wasn't sure, but thought it was mostly ham. A couple of days later, over a lunch of Spam and potato soup, she triumphantly told us, "I was right. Dalia Steffen's cousin in Minnesota is engaged to a man who works for Hormel and she says that he says it means 'spiced ham.'"

By the next day Steve and I, after hours of collaboration, were ready.

"I think it means 'semi-putrid almost-meat,'" Steve said, rolling a Spam meatball around on his plate with a spoon.

Mom stared at him, too surprised to even scold him for not appreciating the food on the table.

"No, it's 'substance posing as meat,'" I spoke up.

Mom started to laugh.

"Squirrel parts and morsels," shouted Steve.

"Sheep pancreas and . . . and . . ." I'd forgotten the rest.

"Mulch," Steve whispered out of the side of his mouth.

Mom put up her hands and called a halt to the proceedings. But she also promised to hold back on the Spam.

For the next couple of years I continued to wear my cousin Herman's hand-me-down cardigans, and Steve got what was left over. Though Mom did prepare Spam less often, she still believed in its nutritional value and continued to prepare Spam sandwiches on a regular basis. She'd slice it thin and slip it between pieces of her homemade bread, attempting to disguise it with lettuce leaves, slices of cheese or bread and butter pickles. Steve and I carried lunch boxes to school that later revealed sandwiches of Spam and mustard, Spam and fried egg, occasionally even Spam and peanut butter. That was better than it sounds.

The war eventually ended, we celebrated Dad's return home and we, along with the rest of the country, moved from rationing to gradual prosperity. Steve and I got new clothes for school. A tiny black and white television took up a place of honor in our living room. Spam all but disappeared from the menu.

Until about twenty years later. Married and the father of two boys, one day I spotted a familiar blue and yellow can on the grocery store shelf and tossed it into the cart with my wife's selections. That weekend I opened the can, fried the slices with some eggs, and served the meal to my family. The reaction was mixed. My wife didn't care for it.

My sons were indifferent, probably just thinking it was oddly-shaped ham.

I thought it was pretty good. I might even try it with some peanut butter.

**Patrick Hoffman** took his family to the Spam Museum in Austin, Minnesota, where he was impressed by the wide range of flavors in which the product is now available. He and his wife Lavinia are the parents of two grown sons and grandparents to four boys.

We thought you'd like to know that one of your customers, _____ _____ has entered the Spam Jingle Contest, a feature of the new Spam programs now heard over WCCO, Minneapolis and St. Paul each Tuesday, Thursday and Saturday afternoon from 5:00 until 5:15 o'clock.

Spam, the new Hormel meat of many uses for many occasions, is winning favor among more and more women every day. You'll find it profitable to feature this sensational new product.

GEO. A. HORMEL & CO.
Austin, Minnesota.

Sketch by LaVonne M. Hansen

Photo provided by Nikole Hall

# A PLACE CALLED . . . OKOBOJI?

## Nikole Hall

Most kids consider the yearly family vacation as something of an adventure. My family, however, took that sense of adventure to extremes. At least our dad did.

Wherever we went, it had to be within two days' driving distance of our home in central Illinois. We couldn't afford plane tickets for all six of us, time was limited, and we didn't want to spend most of our vacation in a car, getting to our destination only to turn around and come back.

So each year, in early June, we went to the map taped to the paneled wall of the basement family room. There was an area circled on the map in thick red crayon. Dad faced the map, got a mental picture of it, then closed his eyes right before slinging a dart at it.

This sometimes produced pretty good results. When I was eight, Dad's dart directed us north, into Canada. None of us had been there before, and it was an adventure of beautiful countryside and accents that seemed strange to us.

There were also some trips that turned out to be less than desirable. When I was nine, Dad's dart directed us to Erie, Pennsylvania. Actually his dart took us to the middle of Lake Erie, and at that time, in the mid-sixties, the lake was at its most polluted. We arrived to see smoke stacks of pollutants spilling into the air, making my sister Jeannie's eyes water and all of us cough like inhabitants of a TB ward.

But our most memorable vacation came three years after the Lake Erie debacle. My twin brothers, Joe and Gary, were thirteen and big for their age, Jeannie was fifteen and I was the youngest at twelve. Dad, eyes shut tight, threw his dart. We all rushed forward to see where we'd be going this time. Jeannie immediately expressed dismay.

"Iowa?" she cried. "What are we going to do in Iowa? Watch corn grow?"

I have to admit I shared her sentiment. Even Mom, who usually tried to put on a game face for Dad's adventures, looked worried. "Maybe you should throw it again, Frank," she murmured.

But Dad was stubborn. "You all know the rules. No do-overs."

Ever dramatic, Jeannie shrieked something about her life being over, ran up the basement steps and to her room, where she slammed the door hard enough to shake the rafters over our heads.

Mom took a closer look at the map. "There's several lakes there," she said. She pulled the dart out and Dad pointed to where it had left its mark. "That's an interesting word," he said. "It looks like . . . Ahck-ah-badg-gee." He rubbed his hands together. "Okay, gang, that's where we're going this year. Pack your swimsuits and bug spray, we're headed for Iowa!"

Over the next few days we prepared for the trip. The drive would take one full day, about nine hours. Dad mapped our route while Mom prepared nutritious sandwiches and snacks.

Finally Saturday arrived, the first day of our vacation. The old Bel Air station wagon, which had seemed so roomy only a few years earlier, now felt cramped. Mom and Dad sat in the front seat of course, with Joe and Gary taking up all the space in the back seat. That meant Jeannie and I were squeezed into the rear compartment with all the luggage, food, reading material, pillows, cameras and various inflatable beach toys. I was jammed into a space the size of our mailbox, yet Jeannie kept elbowing me in the small of the back while saying, "Will you move *over*?"

We traveled through Illinois, then through countless small towns in Iowa, some seeming no more than a blip on our radar. Late that evening we pulled into the parking lot of the motel in what was called the Iowa Great Lakes region.

By morning we were eager to explore. The twins dragged their inner tube down to the water's edge, and Jeannie tried on her new swimsuit, a two-piece she'd bought with her babysitting money. When Dad saw it he choked on his coffee and told her to go put on her one-piece. Sobbing that her life was ruined, Jeannie ran into the tiny room she and I were sharing and slammed the door. I pounded on it, yelling that I needed my swimsuit, until she finally cracked open the door just far enough to fling it at me.

We soon learned there was more to do than just watch corn grow in this popular vacation spot, as well as the correct pronunciation—*Oak*-uh-boje-ee.

There was an amusement park near the water, something called the Tipsy-House, and I met a girl named Dottie, who was from Minnesota and also vacationing with her family. Together we dug for clams along the sandy beaches and rode on the wooden roller-coaster until we were both green and had to sit down with our heads between our knees.

Jeannie met a boy who believed her when she told him she was going to be a senior in the fall, and they made plans to go to a dance at the Roof Garden on Friday night.

Dad became fascinated by some old log cabin and filled our heads with stories about an Indian uprising.

By the time Friday rolled around, we were all feeling sad that this wonderful vacation was nearing an end. We were having way too much fun. Dottie and I were riding the Ferris wheel when the sky grew dark and a sudden wind came up. The ride operator started letting everyone off. When it was our turn to hop down, he told us, "Go straight home, girls, there's a storm comin'."

Dottie and I held hands as we ran, but the wind was so strong we could hardly see where we were going. People ran everywhere, seemingly in all different directions. Dottie was yelling something at me, but I couldn't hear her over the roar of what sounded like a train bearing down on us.

The next thing I knew, a man in an army uniform grabbed both of us in his strong arms, lifting us like we weighed nothing at all. He tossed us through the open doorway of a small diner we'd been in just that morning, and followed us inside where we joined a dozen other people huddled in the ladies' room.

It seemed to last forever. The building shook as though it was going to come down on top of us. Dottie and I hugged each other tight, praying.

Then, just as suddenly, it was over. I looked around for the soldier but he'd already left. When Dottie and I ventured outside, blinking in the sunlight, we saw what looked like total devastation all around us.

We learned later that several tornadoes had torn through the lakes area in a little over twenty minutes. The Roof Garden, where Jeannie had planned to attend a dance with the boy she'd met, had been destroyed. The Ferris wheel Dottie and I had been on was a twisted mass of metal leaning against some battered trees.

Mom packed our station wagon in record time, even though we weren't supposed to leave until the next day. We complained and Jeannie cried, but Mom was adamant. She'd had enough.

We had plenty of stories to tell after that vacation of 1968, and even some pictures. Dottie and I stayed in touch until after high school, when we got busy with our lives and moved on.

We recently reconnected, however, when she found me on Facebook. I picked up my phone and punched in the number she'd provided. One of the first things she said to me, after all those years, was "Wasn't that just the *best* time ever?"

**Nikole Evans Hall** is the owner of a bed-and-breakfast in Vermont, where the walls proudly display many enlarged photos of long-ago family vacations. She recently lost her sister Jeannie to breast cancer, which makes memories of their trip to Okoboji, Iowa even more precious.

Photo provided by Nikole Hall

# HOMESICK

## Bonnie Boeck Ewoldt

The trip from Denison to Lake Okoboji was sweltering on that Sunday afternoon in July of 1955. In my apprehensive ten-year-old mind, it was a millions miles long. Sitting in the backseat of my uncle's Buick, I leaned against the open window and let the wind dry my tears as I gazed at the endless rows of fence posts. I wondered why I'd ever let my cousin, Marsha, talk me into this.

Going to Concordia Cub Week at Camp Okoboji sounded like fun months earlier when Pastor Schmidt handed out pamphlets to our Sunday school class at Zion Lutheran Church. I was excited when Marsha asked me to be her cabin mate, and Mom gave permission for me to go to camp. We spent days poring over the brochures and discussing our choices for crafts and sports. After frequent changes of mind between "leather, copper, or paint," and "volleyball, softball, or archery," we finalized our selections and put the registration forms in the mail. Our long wait for summer began.

During the months of planning and days of packing, it never occurred to me that I would actually be leaving home. Now, speeding along Highway 71 on the way to Okoboji, I was panicky! I'd never seen Lake Okoboji. I'd never been to a camp. In fact, I'd seldom been away from home overnight! How could I survive a week without my family? Even worse, how would my family—my mom and dad—survive a week *without me*?

Eventually, after two long, sweaty, miserable hours, we arrived at the camp entrance, crossed the bridge, and drove up the winding driveway. To me, Camp Okoboji looked like a small town with all of the brown cabins scattered about, connected by winding roads and dirt paths. We parked near the main building where the sight of a long line of children and parents waiting to register traumatized me further. My silent weeping turned into wailing. Somehow, Aunt Helen calmed me down enough to get through the line and registered.

Our cards said "Cabin 18," and the Buick crept along the dirt road through the campground until we found it. We unloaded our belongings from the trunk and carried them into the cabin. My eyes were big and my knees weak as I walked the short hallway that divided the cabin into two rustic sleeping rooms with four bunk beds in each. Back home, I had the entire upstairs of the farmhouse to myself; now I realized I would be sharing a strange bedroom with seven other girls.

I soon learned I would not only be sharing a bedroom, I would be sharing a shower! Two small bathrooms were in the cabin, but we would be taking showers in the Shower House. The thought of walking to another building to take a shower was scary, but the actual idea of showering was terrifying because I'd only used a bathtub at home. By now, I knew staying at Camp Okoboji was going to be anything but the fun adventure we'd planned.

Aunt Helen sensed my distress, but knew I needed to stay. She gave me a hug and said a hasty "Good-bye," with reassurances that I would be just fine. Sadly, I watched Uncle Sam and Aunt Helen drive away. Marsha and I went back into the cabin and decided who would have the top and bottom bunks. She wanted the top bunk, which was fine with me, as the bottom bunk looked much safer. We made our beds and unpacked. Once settled, my gregarious cousin wanted to tour the campgrounds. I just wanted to hide in my hot, stuffy, bottom bunk and cry. After several attempts to get me involved, she finally gave up and went exploring with new friends. When everyone was gone, I worked myself into a pitiful state, convinced I'd never to see home again.

It wasn't long before a counselor heard my sobs and befriended me. When the supper bell rang, she led the girls from our cabin to the dining hall. Inside, three hundred campers sat close together at long tables, laughing, eating, and having wonderful time. I cried through the meal, barely able to swallow any food because of the giant lump in my throat. I missed Mom and Dad so much, and I just knew they were equally miserable back home.

I cried myself to sleep that night and sniffled my way through chapel, crafts, Bible study, sports, and meals the next day. I even cried at the beach during swim time! Marsha long since gave up trying to help and left me to my misery while she had fun with the other kids. The counselors were busy with hundreds of campers, and I felt lonely and abandoned. The first day at camp was the most miserable day of my young life and I was sure I would die of homesickness. Once again, I cried myself to sleep in my suffocating bottom bunk and thought the week would never end. I desperately wanted to go home.

My counselor could do nothing to console me, so the next morning after breakfast she left me at the nurse's cabin. The camp nurse checked me over and determined there was nothing physically wrong. She then pointed to a chair and told me to sit down and cry. I was stunned! Cry? Just sit there and cry? In my bewildered state, I noticed another girl sitting in a nearby chair, hugging her knees and crying. She seemed even more miserable than I was! After a rather awkward greeting, I learned her name was Mary. She said she wanted to go home. I told her I wanted to go home, too.

We talked about our homes and families. The conversation drifted to crafts at camp and we discovered we were both in "Copper." Soon, we were laughing about the counselors' skits and stunts by our cabin mates. After a short while, we left the nurse's cabin and ran to catch up with the other campers.

That night, I was exhausted and drifted off to sleep without crying.

Waves of homesickness returned occasionally during the remainder of the week, but they didn't last long because I was caught up in the excitement of camp life. Not only did I survive my week at camp, I later remembered it as the best week of my life. I excitedly returned for Concordia Cub Week the next two summers.

Ironically, fifty years later, my home is located three miles from Camp Okoboji. For many summers, I worked on the camp staff and registered thousands of campers over the years. My favorites were the young, first-timers who came to camp from all over Iowa and Minnesota. When they arrived with their families on Sunday afternoons, they looked at me with apprehensive eyes. I always smiled at them and spoke from the heart when I said, "Welcome to Camp Okoboji! You're going to have a wonderful time!"

**Bonnie Boeck Ewoldt** outgrew her tendency toward homesickness and now finds traveling to new destinations one of her favorite pastimes. More of Bonnie's humorous and inspirational writing can be found on her blog: www.bonniesblogbox.wordpress.com.

Photo provided by Chris Devaney

Photo used with permission of
KELO-TV in Sioux Falls, South Dakota.

# WATERSKIING WITH CAPTAIN 11

## Judy Taber

S ummertime vacations at Lake Okoboji in northwest Iowa seemed to be out of the question for our family. I guess we lived too close to it. Consequently, it held a special pull for me as I was growing up. Mom and Dad would take us to Arnolds Park Amusement Park located on the east shore once each summer, where my brother and I could go on several rides. That was the extent of our vacationing there. More often, we would take a week in early August to vacation and visit relatives somewhere else. I got to go to Oregon, North Dakota, Saskatchewan and Ontario, Canada, Niagara Falls, the Black Hills, and the Rocky Mountains. But the lake still called.

So imagine my delight when the 4-H club leaders decided to take all twelve members of the Excelsior Everlasting Echoes 4-H club for an outing at Lake Okoboji. Fillenwarth Beach Resort, just north of the amusement park, owned an old two-story house in addition to the many units they rented out. For a very reasonable price, our 4-H club rented the completely furnished house for two days. As part of our learning experience, we took food with us to cook our meals.

When we weren't cooking, cleaning, or working on 4-H projects, we would go swimming in Lake Okoboji. What a treat that was!

On our second afternoon at the beach, a boat came up to the dock. There were six people on board, and we realized that one of the men was a celebrity.

Dave Dedrick, also known as Captain 11, was the weatherman at KELO TV in Sioux Falls, South Dakota. He also hosted an after-school program for kids called, of course, *Captain 11*. Mounted on the wall behind the Captain was a box-like structure about four feet high and eight feet long. Made from an old pinball machine with bells and lights and relay switches, it was known as the Time-Converter. When Captain 11 pushed the buttons, it made noise and the lights flashed.

As it came time for a cartoon, the camera would zoom in on the Twerlitzer Wheel, a flat disc with a spiral line that spun with hypnotic effect as the camera drew closer and closer. We thought it was wonderful.

The Captain 11 Show had a special introduction each day. In his book, *It Ain't All Cartoons*, Dave Dedrick recounted those words:

> *Captain 11 . . . Today's man of the future.*
> *One man in each century is given the power*
> *to control time.*
>
> *The man chosen to receive this power is*
> *carefully selected.*
> *He must be kind . . . he must be fair . . . he*
> *must be brave.*
>
> *You have fulfilled these requirements, and*
> *We of the outer galaxies designate to you*
> *The wisdom of Solomon And the strength of*
> *Atlas.*
>
> *You are Captain 11.*

He dressed the part, too. Captain 11 wore a blue jumpsuit, and the aviator scarf wrapped around his neck had an "11" on it. With the wide belt, pilot's cap and set of earphones, he really looked like a captain.

That summer day, as the boat pulled up to the Fillenwarth dock, Captain 11 shouted, "Any of you girls want to go water skiing?"

"Yes!" I shouted back.

Most of the other adults got out of the boat. Some of my friends got in with Captain 11 and one other man. They tossed short, wide skis and a life jacket to me. After I put them on I floated in the water, where they threw out the tow rope and circled around me until I could grab it.

Then away we went!

I was almost up, and then I was back in the water. They circled around again so I could grab the rope. Leaning over the side of the boat, Captain 11 told me what I had done wrong and how to correct it.

With the next try, I got up. What an exhilarating feeling it was, to be skimming along on top of the water as the boat pulled me along. After making several big circles in the water in front of the resort, Captain 11 and the other man drove the boat slowly in close to the dock where I let go of the tow rope.

I was so excited. I had gotten up on water skis and Captain 11 had piloted the boat. I could hardly wait to tell Mom and Dad. I soon graduated to longer, narrower skis. Streaking across the water at a high rate of speed was great fun. I owe many wonderful memories to the kindness of a man who loved kids and took time out of his vacation to teach me.

**Judy Taber**, a retired adjunct university professor, and her husband, Gary, live in the home they built on the south shore of Silver Lake at Lake Park, Iowa. Depending on the season and/or weather, she can be found working in her gardens or creating stained and fused glass art.

The Patch/Eeten House
Hartley, Iowa

# BACKYARD MEMORIES

## Jane Kauzlarich

I spent my childhood in and around a massive three-story Victorian house in small-town northwest Iowa. Having moved there from a small bungalow on the other side of town, nearly a mile away, we called it "The Big House." Lightning rods adorned the peaked roof, and the dusty attic had round windows on all four sides. It was a treasure, especially when we children would navigate the narrow wooden stairs and creaking rafters to scan the horizon.

With the other neighborhood children we played Red Rover, Red Rover, Come Over, Come Over on the green expanse of our front lawn, frolicking until after dark, gazing at moths that we called "millers," which gathered at the front porch light.

The delivery man brought glass bottles of milk, and placed them at our front door by dawn. Mom would call the grocery store with her order of staples, which were delivered to our back door by the kitchen. This was our mother's domain, complete with flour bin and pantry. It was a simple time . . . with simple pleasures.

In the back yard, we climbed the ancient maple tree and played hide and seek in the raspberry patch. With the help of our cocker spaniel and pet crow, my sister and I picked the berries and sold them for forty cents a pint, eighty cents a quart.

We had a vegetable cave which also served as a tornado shelter. My sister taught me to ride my blue one-speed Schwinn by pushing me down from that mound. It seemed like a mountain to me as I gained seemingly incredible speed, careening wildly toward the neighbors' garden.

There were wonderful old red barns behind our property . . . wood, of course. I was fascinated by them. We weren't actually allowed in those rustic barns. But my best friend and I trespassed anyway, crawling around in the hay, often unearthing interesting items. Once we found a dead cat and took it to the high school science teacher several blocks up our long street. He said, "It's a dead cat...now get it out of here!" He was accustomed to our visits, but wasn't pleased on that occasion.

My friend and I would hide in the raspberry patch when the elderly farmer slowly made his way down the path that bordered the entire neighborhood, adjacent to a golden field of corn. He'd say to my father, "Those girls have been in the barns again." My father, an adventurer himself, never scolded us for this misdemeanor. He knew we were entranced by the pigeons, thick ropes, leather horse collars and other artifacts of rural life.

Our family had banty chickens that lived in the biggest barn. They were tame, and would roost on our shoulders and arms. The rooster we called "Roosty" a.k.a. "Benny." The hen was "Henny." They enriched our lives, providing us with eggs and yellow chicks. Eventually Roosty and Henny returned to their original locale just north of the grade at Big Spirit Lake. Farm life in the city limits!

Our parents allowed us to have turtles, parakeets, chameleons from the Shrine Circus in Sioux City, plus numerous cats. Sometimes the felines would climb the mulberry bush to my brother's bedroom on the second floor where, hearing their meows, he opened the window so they could sleep with him. We were blessed.

When our father let us dig a fox hole in the backyard we played Army and took turns wearing a World War I helmet. It was authentic, complete with a deep bullet dent.

The tracks of the Milwaukee Railroad were a half-mile south of The Big House. My friend and I explored the haunts of hobos, common in those days. We found campfires, mattresses, and empty tin cans. My mother provided the vagabonds with sandwiches and angel food cake, but I'm certain neither she nor my father knew of our surreptitious trips to the tracks.

The house had three porches. On the side porch I placed my collection of insects in glass jars. I tended my captives carefully. My sister and I, along with my childhood pal, performed Romeo and Juliet there for our neighbors and playmates.

We also had "bicycle rodeos" and even a little café called The Brown Derby, located in my friend's playhouse. Our mothers provided the brownies and pies. We donated our proceeds—$13.67—to the new hospital in our thriving small town. We were adolescent entrepreneurs, selling comic books and advertising with colored chalk on the sidewalks along our street.

We called ourselves "The Good Citizens' Club," of which we two were the only members. We had a secret hand signal and a password: "Zoo-be-zee." We kept minutes at our meetings and detailed ideas for future escapades. We performed pantomimes to 45 records, entertaining at ladies' clubs and church societies. "Sylvester and Tweetie," and "Mutual Admiration Society" were our favorites.

Those were the days. They were innocent times, with back yard memories forever in my heart.

**Jane Hansen Kauzlarich** is a native of Hartley, Iowa. She grew up loving animals of all kinds. After being a business and English teacher for thirty-six years, she currently volunteers for a wildlife rehabilitator and a no-kill dog/cat shelter. In her retirement she enjoys reading, writing poetry and essays, biking, hiking, fishing, and playing guitar, banjo, and drums.

# FOUND!

## Debra Dunn Kaczmarek

**P**erhaps because we lacked most of the finer things in life, we five Dunn kids developed meaningful relationships with the ubiquitous rural dumps of our day. Predecessors of today's sanitary landfill, though with considerably less emphasis on the *sanitary*, these dumps sprouted at many intersections of the gravel roads that carved Northwest Iowa farm country into tidy squares like pieces of a giant sheet cake. Dumps were the final resting places for rusted silage buckets, discarded appliances, worn-out tires, corrugated sheet metal—anything that was too large for, or otherwise unsuited to, the farmyard junk piles.

*Our* dumps—the one at the southwest corner of our property where Willow Creek separated our "bottom" field from Steffens' cow pasture, and the far grander one located just across from the Schutknechts' farmstead—were superior to most dumps in that they were self-cleaning. The former was situated on one bank of Willow Creek, which could be counted on to flood spectacularly every spring and carry the detritus of our lives to places far downstream. We liked to think of our discarded snow fence ending up in a Louisiana bayou where an assembled throng would speculate as to its origin and purpose.

The Schutknecht dump was without peer. It was located on a bluff high above Willow Creek, which had spent eons carving its way through our part of the county, creating hills and valleys and other geological features not frequently encountered in northwest Iowa. The farmers who utilized this particular dump were apparently a daring bunch, for they deposited their refuse alarmingly close to the edge of the bluff. Periodically, large portions of the bluff would give way, sending good Iowa loam and our cast-offs into the creek. If these landslides occurred when the creek was running sluggishly, the quality of our summer recreation was compromised. We didn't mind cavorting in water laced with cow manure and blood suckers, but we didn't much fancy swimming with rusty barbed wire and rolling coulters.

In the mid-twentieth century, folks didn't often throw away items that had any usefulness remaining, so it's not surprising that despite years of scavenging we rarely found anything worth bringing home. I remember being extremely excited when we found four or five antique irons—a few that had to be heated on a wood stove and one that had an attached receptacle that hung at half-mast behind the handle. We figured it for an early steam iron, but it turns out that the battered little tank was intended for gas that fueled the contraption. Mom wasn't impressed, and even dear Grandma Bobzien dampened our enthusiasm by confessing that she'd thrown out dozens of such irons as soon as she could afford a "mod-run" one. Thoroughly discouraged, we tossed the irons into our attic where they remained, no doubt, until the house was razed.

Sadly, the same fate almost certainly met our most memorable find, the one true treasure we ever claimed from any dump.

All our lives, we kids had longed for a piano. Dad's musical gift had wriggled its way into our DNA, and we were fine singers. We figured that we might be pretty fair instrumentalists, too, if only we had the means by which to acquire the requisite musical instrument. Dad's sister, Aunt Alice, was reputed to have taught herself to play piano and organ by ear, so we figured we could circumvent the whole teacher-lessons thing by becoming pianists. Alas, pianos cost money. And we had no money.

Then, one day, as we were riding the afternoon school bus home from Rossie, we passed the Schutknecht dump and were thunderstruck by the changes the day had wrought. A fresh load of junk had been deposited, and there, perched majestically, if a little off-kilter, amid smoldering tractor tires and broken sauerkraut crocks, was a magnificent upright piano. God had answered my prayers. Here was a piano we could afford—free for the taking.

It was clear, however, that the taking wouldn't be easy. Already, flames were licking at the carved base of the blue-painted instrument. Time was clearly of the essence. But, wouldn't you know it, Mom and Dad were away doing field work for hire at a property near St. James, Minnesota.

Fortunately, my brother Butch was always eager to operate machinery. As soon as we'd raced home, all of us running the entire way up our half-mile lane, he fired up the little Ford tractor equipped with a front loader. The rest of us—still in our school clothes—leapt into the bucket of the loader for the full-throttle ride down our hilly, rutted lane and back up the hilly, rutted road to Schutknechts' dump.

We bailed out of the loader, and stepping gingerly to avoid hot spots and sharp edges, we made our way over to the piano. It didn't look so fine close up, frankly. The ivory had been pried from the keys, and the blue paint was chipped in lots of places. Worst of all, the dump fire had raised some havoc with one side. But the wood was just smoking; there was no sign of active fire.

So I signaled Butch to approach. He drove over perhaps twenty feet of assorted debris—all of it flirting with the idea of bursting into flame—before lowering the bucket and beginning the tricky business of working the lip of it under the edge of the piano. The rest of us got behind the piano and tried to tip it into the loader while avoiding contact with anything lethal.

Pianos are heavy—especially old uprights. We couldn't budge the thing, so Butch goosed the Ford a bit in order to force the bucket under the piano. It was too much of a good thing, for suddenly the piano threatened to fall back on us.

47

I have no recollection of how we managed to reverse the piano's course and coax it into that loader. I only know that we were not crushed to death and that we held that massive piano in the pint-sized loader all the way home—over all those fiendish ruts—and managed somehow to maneuver the behemoth instrument into the house.

I've forgotten not only the most harrowing moments in our Great Piano Rescue, but I also draw a complete blank when it comes to calling up any memory of Mom and Dad's reaction to the sudden appearance of a big blue piano in the house. Surely they noticed!

My sister Sue says that a piano makes a home. I agree. Certainly, I felt that we were better people for having a piano of our own. Still, candor requires that I admit our instrument's shortcomings. It reeked, for one thing. It had a bone-deep stink to it—the sort of rancid mustiness you find in old books that have been stored in damp cellars. But with notes of burning garbage.

Unfortunate—and persistent—as the odor problem was, the piano had a bigger flaw: the keys that did operate produced a disappointingly tinny sound. After what we'd gone through to get our piano, I couldn't bring myself to speak of this imperfection. But the truth is that our instrument sounded just like the honky-tonk pianos in the saloons on TV westerns.

Growing up in Northwest Iowa, **Deb Kaczmarek** dreamed of becoming a famous soprano—or maybe a Pulitzer Prize-winning novelist. Turns out that she has (thus far) achieved fame only as the Egg Lady of St. Isidore Farm, where her eighty beautiful hens labor under the supervision of Bertrand, the happiest rooster in the hemisphere.

Photo provided by Karen Howard

# MAMA'S SEWING MACHINE

## Karen Fields Carr

Growing up in rural Iowa provided a wide array of opportunities and experiences. Among them were the times my mother spent at her treadle sewing machine. She could really make that old Singer hum. Coming home from school, my brother and I would usually find her seated in front of her machine. She was a miracle-maker, creating fantastic memories for all of us.

In those days, a farm wife needed to be extremely frugal and my mother was indeed that. The feed we used on the farm came in cotton bags. Some of the designs were quite nice and could be made into wonderful garments and other practical items. Mom made stacks of dishtowels and many aprons from these colorful feed sacks. They also provided great opportunities for a young and budding seamstress to learn how to sew, and who better for a teacher than one who did it so well?

My mother even created several two-piece sun suits for me out of the plain colored sacks. Then there were sacks with charcoal and green patterns that had a kind of denim look to them. From those she made matching shorts for my little brother. We were the best-dressed kids, and no one was the wiser that our outfits came from feed sacks!

I still have a double-wedding-ring quilt, which my mother made out of feed sacks and other fabric remnants. Yes, Mom was also an avid quilter. After piecing together the many parts, she would place it on the quilt frame, draw her own designs and begin the actual quilting. She made many quilts for her children, their spouses, and for each of her five grandchildren. Once she was honored to have a lady from Chicago hire her to make a quilt out of her husband's silk neckties. Mom enjoyed the challenge, but had a hard time finding silk thread for the project. Spencer, Iowa just didn't carry much of that sort of thing back then.

Mom's quilting was well known throughout Clay County. She showed several of her quilts at the Clay County Fair, and she also demonstrated quilting on a small frame at the Albert City Thresher's Show for several years. The small frame was one that my dad had made for her before that sort of thing actually became popular.

Another special memory for me was when I was in first grade at Gillette Grove Consolidated School and had been chosen to be the flower girl for Homecoming. Out of a plain feed sack, Mom made a simple, sleeveless, floor-length under-slip. From some old gauzy-like curtain panels she made an over-dress with puffy sleeves and a long tie. She then dyed both a bright, springy yellow. It was the nicest dress, and I was so proud to wear it. I just never shared that it was made out of our old living room curtains!

Now it's something I remember with pride.

Mom would even design her own patterns, which she cut out of newspaper. If I had found a store-bought garment I liked, she would make a pattern just by looking at it and sew me a new garment. Sometimes she borrowed a garment to make the pattern. She taught me to do this as well, and I was able to give a 4-H demonstration on how to design a pattern and make a blouse.

I do believe Mom could have been a top designer had she been given the chance. As it was, I was the recipient of some pretty classy clothes.

Our home was filled with her sewing creations. She made curtains for every room in the house as well as chair pad covers, couch slipcovers, and toss pillows. She also created unique cross-stitch items. Her embroidery designs gave an elegant quality to the plain feed-sack dishtowels.

Fortunately for me, I was the main recipient of her delightful creations. She made shirts for my brother when he was little, but she continued creating beautiful and unique articles of clothing for me throughout my high school years.

Thanks, Mom. I'm sure at the time I never showed you the proper appreciation for all the fantastic sewing you did for me. But in retrospect, I had it pretty darned good.

**Karen Fields Carr** lives in Mason City, Iowa, where she has recently retired after thirty-two years at Mercy Medical Center-North Iowa. Her first children's book, *The Many Hats of Jeremiah Porter* was published in 2010, and two other children's books will soon come out. Her mother, children and grandchildren have been a rich source of inspiration in her writing. She is currently working on a novel honoring her mother.

Photo provided by Karen Jones Schutt

# THE SAGA OF THE PEACHES

## Karen Jones Schutt

Grandpa and Grandma had a hard time of it raising four boys in the late thirties on a rocky Missouri farm. There was never enough to go around, whether it be food, clothing, or good fortune. They did their best, and somehow managed to keep body and soul together for everyone in the family.

One summer Grandpa heard there was a truckload of peaches in town that could be bought for a song. The wheels started turning and soon he had those green and hard peaches purchased and loaded into the old truck.

"I can take them up north to Iowa and peddle them. They probably don't have peaches yet this early, so I should be able to sell them. The two young'uns can go along and smile real nice and win over the ladies. You two older ones can stay home and be the men of the family and do the chores."

The two older boys grumbled a bit, but knew the law had been laid down. Grandma and Grandpa quickly gathered together a camping outfit, some quilts, extra clothing, bacon, flour, and a few potatoes. The peaches were covered with canvas and they were off, rattling and banging up the road to Iowa. They were in a hurry, and would need to sell the peaches before they got too ripe.

The little boys were excited to be on an adventure and tried to take in everything they saw. This was their first long trip away from home.

"Are we about there yet?" one of them asked after an hour on the road.

"We aren't even out of Missouri," answered their father.

That evening, just inside the Iowa border, they found a grassy place and set up camp. Soon Grandpa had a fire going and potatoes frying. They were just about the best fried potatoes the boys had ever eaten.

Late the next day Grandpa thought they were far enough north to find some good markets. They pulled into a small town and set up shop. They sold a few, hardly making a dent in the load. The little boys smiled shyly and attracted a few customers, but Grandpa hoped the next day would be better.

They moved on early, and over the week hit several towns. It was always the same, the boys smiled at the ladies and a few peaches were sold. They took in enough to buy gas and little more.

After a week, Grandpa observed that the remaining peaches were looking a little wilted and most were dead ripe. He decided to turn south and head back to Missouri.

Everyone was disappointed in the venture except the little boys; they'd had a wonderful time. School would be starting and there was little money for new shoes and overalls. They would make do, as they always had.

Grandpa was all set to shovel the peaches to the hogs and save some pig feed. "At least they all won't go to waste," he said, "and they might even make some good-tasting pork."

"Wait!" said Grandma. "Not so fast! Let me pick out the best ones and I'll can them. Can't let them all go to the pigs."

So Grandma rounded up some canning jars, lids, and precious sugar to save what peaches she could. It was broiling in the kitchen, over the hot cook stove as she canned them, but the rows of filled jars, all golden on the table, promised sweet desserts come fall and winter.

"No loss without some gain," said Grandpa.

"Mighty small gain, if you ask me," retorted Grandma, wiping away the sweat.

The next day the jars were carried to the cool cellar and forgotten. But not for long. Several nights later the entire family was awakened by gunshots in the cellar. The gunshots were not all at once, but spaced over an hour or so.

"Someone's stealing our peaches!" hollered one of the little boys.

Grandpa quickly realized what the racket was all about. "Nobody's stealing the peaches," he said. "It's not gunshots, the jars are exploding. They were too ripe and must have fermented."

Grandma was almost ready to cry when she surveyed the mess the next morning. "All that sugar gone to waste," she lamented. Grandpa mentioned all the hard and hot work for nothing.

The boys noticed a wonderful yeasty, peachy scent in the air.

"Well, boys, find some buckets and we'll scoop it all up and empty the jars. The pigs will like these peaches even better because they're sweet."

With everyone working, the mess was soon cleaned up. Grandma washed the few jars that hadn't broken and the lids. The boys scrubbed and walls, the floor, the shelves and wiped off everything that had been splattered by fermenting peach juice. Now there would be no sweet peaches for a treat come winter, no golden juice to spoon up. It was a sober day.

Grandma fixed the noon meal and the boys worked in the garden. Grandpa put away all the camping gear and life returned to normal. But not for long.

Around the middle of the afternoon, the littlest boy came shrieking to the house. "There's something awful wrong with the pigs, just come and see."

Everyone stopped what they were doing and ran out to the pig pen. What they saw stunned them all. Some of the pigs were lying on their backs, lazily moving their legs back and forth. Some were leaning against the fence and making a sort of hiccupping sound. A few fell over as they tried to walk. Many were making a mournful oiiin...kk-ing sound.

Grandpa started laughing.

Grandma said, "I don't see what's so funny! They must be sick!"

Grandpa kept on laughing. "They're not sick, they're DRUNK!" he said. "They're all drunk on fermented peaches."

Soon the boys were rolling on the ground and laughing at the sight of intoxicated pigs.

Grandpa and the boys scooped out what was left of the peaches, but the pigs had done a good job of cleaning them up. They all couldn't stop laughing, except for Grandma.

She stomped back to the house, fuming. "Is there no end to my earthly woes? It's not enough to keep men and boys away from the drink, now I have to keep the pigs away too!"

**Karen Jones Schutt** and her husband, Charles, live in the best place possible: the hills of the Big Sioux River, near Sioux Falls, South Dakota. Her hobbies include gazing across the valley with coffee cup in hand, writing about her childhood in the 1940s, quilting, keeping track of her four grandkids, and traveling to visit her far-flung children. Canning peaches is not on the list.

Sketch by LaVonne M. Hansen

# MY BROTHER'S CAR

## Daisy McCauley

I was called the tag-along in the family, because I was born when my parents were in their early forties. By the time I was in kindergarten I was already an aunt to my older sister's two kids, and my brother Jerry was in high school.

Tall and handsome, Jerry could fix anything, and wasn't afraid to get his hands dirty or to crawl under the family car to find where that knocking was coming from. I would kneel on the ground next to his tool box, ready to pass him whichever tool he asked for. I learned the names of all of Jerry's tools. I could tell the difference between a fine tooth ratchet wrench and a torque wrench, as well as a Phillips and a flat-head screwdriver.

In his sophomore year, Jerry picked up an old late-fifties Ford for a song. He and a couple of friends towed it to our house, where they pushed it the rest of the way into the back yard and next to the garage. Seeing it, Mom just shook her head and retreated back into the house, mumbling, ". . . going to start looking like a junkyard around here, I can just see it."

That spring, between school, baseball practice and his part-time job, Jerry began working on the car. I was never far away.

"Pass me the locking pliers, Daisy," Jerry said, only the bottom half of him sticking out from under the car. One hand snaked out, fingers spread, as he waited for me to do my part.

I located the pliers quickly in his neatly-arranged red metal toolbox, and slapped them into his palm like a nurse handing a scalpel to the surgeon.

I would have happily spent every weekend there in the back yard with my brother, but Mom wasn't having it. When she came out one Saturday to find both my brother's long legs and my short, overall-clad ones sticking out from under the car, she grabbed me by the ankles and pulled me out into the sunlight. "Young lady, you're coming with me to Aunt Fern's for afternoon tea," she told me.

"Noooooo!" I wailed as Mom dragged me into the house. I knew what she was up to. My Aunt Fern, Mom's sister, had spent a couple of years "abroad," as she called it, and had come back with airs that included afternoon teas at which I would be forced to wear a dress and my best Sunday shoes. Whenever I got particularly down and dirty, Mom tried to feminize me with a couple of hours of culture.

It took nearly an hour in the bath to get the grease out of my hair and the dirt from under my fingernails. But finally, with me dressed in a pink organza dress and black Mary Janes, we walked the five blocks to my aunt's place.

"Oh, precious, you look just adorable!" my aunt exclaimed, throwing her hands in the air. To my mother she added, "You are a miracle worker." As though I were a stray mutt that had been cleaned up and transformed into a show dog. Which was sort of what I felt like.

I endured the tea, trying not to spill any of it on myself as they talked over my head about my sister Iris and her two adorable children who had never fallen face-first into a puddle or torn the knees of their blue jeans.

When we got home later I changed back into my overalls and ran out the back door. I crouched down by the car and Jerry called out, "Hand me that oil pan, will ya, Daize?" as though I hadn't even been gone.

By mid-summer Jerry had the car up and running. When he took me out for the first test run, I knew it was his way of thanking me for all my help. The Ford never did look terrific, but he spruced it up as best he could and it ran great. Jerry drove that car for the next couple of years, until he graduated and joined the navy. When he shipped out it was put in storage, which meant it was covered with a tarp and pushed to a spot behind the garage.

A few years later, when I was in high school myself, Jerry and his wife came home for a visit. He'd stayed in the navy, and the car had stayed behind the garage. When he said, "C'mon, Daize, let's go see how the old Ford's doing," I happily followed him outside. It felt like old times.

Even though it had been inactive, the car hadn't been neglected. At least every six months Dad had started it up, checked the battery and made sure the tires stayed inflated. Together Jerry and I cleaned it up and drove it out onto the driveway.

*He's going to take it with him,* I thought wistfully.

Instead, he handed me the keys.

"Wha . . ." I sputtered.

"It's yours," he said. "I'm going to be a dad in a few months, and this ain't no family car."

I threw my arms around his neck until he started making choking sounds. Then I took the keys and hopped in my car.

For the next several years that car went everywhere with me. It may not have looked like much, but I kept it running like a top. Then one day, after coming out of the shoe store, I turned the key in the ignition and nothing happened. I got out, lifted the hood, and was staring down at the engine when a man about my own age appeared at my side.

"Having some trouble, Miss?" he asked.

I stared up into gorgeous blue eyes and was glad I was wearing my best navy skirt and heels. Mom's early efforts to feminize me hadn't been a complete waste of time. Even so, some things never change. A lesser woman might have simpered and accepted the assistance of this handsome stranger. Not me. I smiled and said, "It's just the battery cables."

I retrieved my toolbox from the backseat of the car, took out a rag to wipe the corrosion off the cables, then used a pliers to tighten them. This time when I turned the key in the ignition, the engine fired right up.

Fortunately for me, my future husband wasn't one bit intimidated by this lack of helplessness on my part. As he said many times over the years, he'd rather have a wife who was self-sufficient than one who needed him to do every little thing for her.

He got that in spades.


Author **Daisy McCauley** took the old Ford with her to college in Mankato, Minnesota, and it stayed with her for the next twenty years, finally racking up an impressive 215,199 miles.

*DAISY MCCAULEY*

# THE NEW CAR

## Janet Branson

It was the fall of 1950. I was nine. The crops were in, the prices were good and our old blue 1940 Dodge was wearing out. My dad didn't want to put any more money into it, afraid that it might break down somewhere and we wouldn't be able to get home. He decided we should buy a new car. It was quite a process going from one car dealer to another looking at their offerings and studying the attributes of each.

In the end he and Mom decided on a 1950 four-door, shiny black Mercury. They made out the order and the salesman sent it in. We anxiously waited for the news of its arrival. It was a long, agonizing wait. All of us were excited, since this was our first new car. Finally the letter came and we dressed up to go to town to bring it home. This new shiny black Mercury was a sight to behold. She was a beauty!

Mom and Daddy were welcomed into the office while my brother, Jerry, and I tried to occupy ourselves in the waiting room. Soon my parents came out with the keys in hand and off we went in our new car. It just glided down the road, almost like riding on a cloud.

At the age of nine I really had little knowledge of high finance, so I asked,

"How much did it cost, Daddy?" He didn't tell me.

"Well, how much money did you get back when you bought it?" I asked. They actually had no idea what I was asking. My point of reference was that when you paid for something with a dollar you usually got change back, and that's what I wanted to know.

"No, Sis, we just gave them the right amount. We didn't get any change," they explained. That was good enough for me.

We'd had it for only a few weeks when I came home from school one afternoon to find my mother in tears. She had looked out the kitchen door and the car was gone. She knew Daddy hadn't taken it anywhere while wearing his work clothes. She stepped outside and there it was in the bottom of the coulee. Someone hadn't set the parking brake and it rolled down the bank. Mom was so sick about it that she cried most of the afternoon. I have no idea how they got it up out of the coulee and into town to be fixed. That 1950 Mercury must have been tough as nails. Evidently it wasn't that badly damaged but Mom sure did cry buckets of tears over it.

The next summer we took it to Oregon to see my mother's aunt. This car served us well for several years until 1958 when we traded it in on an almost-new Pontiac station wagon. It was the first car I learned to drive.

My husband, Bruce, and I bought a new car once ourselves. It was a white, 1967 two-door Pontiac LeMans with a red stripe along the bottom of the doors, and red vinyl interior. It was right off the showroom floor. In just a few weeks we would move from Denver to Hartley. We loved that car. It was so much fun to drive. But as our family expanded with a new baby, we reluctantly traded it in on a copper-colored Rambler station wagon. How exciting.

That Pontiac was evidently a rare model, as we have never seen another one like it. We often wonder what happened to it. Does it still exist? What does it look like if it does? Have the people taken good care of it? Has someone restored it to its former glory?

I'm afraid we will never know the answers to these questions.

**Janet Branson** has lived in Hartley, Iowa for forty-six years. She began writing several years ago when she retired as a school cook. Her main focus is on stories from her childhood and those related to her interest in genealogy in the hope that her children will find them interesting. She is grandmother to twelve beautiful grandchildren who are the light of her life.

# GRANDPA & THE SQUIRRELS

### Kathleen Murray

My grandpa was an animal lover, and he taught me to be one too. One of my earliest memories was when I was only three or four, and he lifted me up on his wide, strong shoulders so I could see into a robin's nest that had been constructed in low branches of an elm tree. There were four blue eggs in the nest. The mother robin, perched on the branch of another tree, scolded us furiously.

"Don't touch the nest, Kat," Grandpa said softly, then lowered me to the ground. "We'll look, but we don't want to disturb it or the mother might decide to abandon it."

He took my hand in his and led me back to the house. Before we had gone more than ten feet, the mother robin swooped down from the tree to her nest, where she settled in.

Grandpa and Grandma's farm was a wonderland of barn cats, chickens and velvet-nosed calves. My dad, mother, older brother Cal and I went there almost every weekend during the summer months.

Grandpa respected all animals. He taught me, by example, to be gentle with the new kittens in the barn. I helped bottle-feed calves and tossed feed to the chickens. When Barney, the cranky old rooster, chased me all the way to the back porch, wings flapping and sharp beak pecking at my heels, Grandpa wiped my tears but reminded me that the yard was Barney's home and I had invaded his territory.

He also taught me which animals not to touch. From a safe distance, and with his old WWI binoculars in hand, we watched as a family of foxes peeked cautiously out from their den, the three pups big-eared and curious.

"They won't hurt us," Grandpa explained patiently. "But if we get too close they might get spooked and move to a different spot, and then we wouldn't have the pleasure of watching them."

The only animals I ever heard Grandpa cuss at were the squirrels. The grove behind the barn was full of them. Most of the time the squirrels minded their own business. But when Cal gave Grandma a pretty bird feeder he'd made for her, the squirrels quickly discovered it.

The bird feeder sat on a platform on a post in the middle of the backyard. Grandma filled it with store-bought feed. With a perfect view of the feeder from her kitchen window, she declared it to be better than television.

Then, one Saturday morning just a week or so later, we all heard her declare, "Oh! That squirrel chased my birds right out of there!"

Mom and I were in the other room, but we hurried to the kitchen and looked out the window over her head. And there we saw them—first one squirrel, then another, sitting on the bird feeder, munching contentedly at the seed. We didn't actually see one of them lift a furry arm and gesture for their friends to join them, but that must have been what happened because even as we watched three more squirrels scampered across the grass, up the wooden pole and onto the platform.

Grandma gasped.

I said, "Oh, cute!"

Then we all heard a string of expletives that could have peeled the paint off the side of the barn. Grandpa, moving as fast as his bad knee would allow, crossed the lawn from the other direction. The squirrels wisely scattered. Some scampered head-first down the pole, others leapt to the ground as though weightless, and before Grandpa reached them they were all back in the grove.

"@#$%^&* varmints!" He shook his fist at the thick growth of trees, but the squirrels had all gone into hiding. "@#$%^&* tree rats!"

Even I, who heard Cal cuss pretty regularly when our parents weren't around, was shocked. Grandma hurried to the screen door, opened it and called, "Vernon, are you forgetting there are young ears in the vicinity?"

Seeing the three of us, now all out on the back porch, Grandpa looked properly chastened and offered an apology. Mumbling under his breath, he headed for the barn.

And thus began the battle of the squirrels. For the rest of that summer Mom, Dad, Cal and I were more eager than ever to get to the farm, to see what new idea Grandpa had come up with to keep the squirrels out of the bird feeder.

First he replaced the wooden pole with a long metal pipe left over from some earlier home project. After the squirrels scampered easily up the pole, he greased it. That seemed to work—for a little while. But before long they were in the feeder again, leaving us to wonder how they were managing it. By hiding in the house and peeking out from behind the curtains, we watched as a squirrel made a nearly unbelievable leap of distance from the low-hanging branch of a tree, onto Grandma's clothesline, which it then traversed upside down with impressive agility until it was within distance of the feeder.

Grandpa and Dad moved the clothesline. The squirrels, like tiny stealth commandos, made their way across the lawn, up the side of the house onto the roof, from where they could jump to the feeder. Moving the feeder farther from the house would only put it closer to the trees, so that wasn't an option.

Then, one Saturday morning, I nearly bumped into Grandpa behind the barn. He was peering down the barrel of his .22, which he had pointed in the direction of the bird feeder. Two squirrels were on the feeder, their paws filled with sunflower seeds, jaws briskly working.

I gasped. Grandpa lowered his rifle and turned slowly to look at me. The expression on my face, I can only imagine, must have been one of horror. He sighed, put his arm around my shoulders, and we walked in silence to the house.

Later that afternoon, Grandpa and I nailed a foot-square wood platform to one of the biggest trees at the edge of the grove. On that platform we placed a couple of ears of corn and a handful of in-the-shell peanuts. For the remainder of the summer I made it my job to see to it that the squirrel feeders always held a supply of treats. It didn't keep them out of the bird feeder entirely, but it made a big difference.

My grandfather may have accepted defeat in that particular battle, but his esteem, in my eyes, rose to even greater heights.

**Kathleen Murray** still lives in Ohio, where she has her own bird feeders and regularly puts out corn for the squirrels. She has four grandchildren and shares with them the lessons of life that her grandparents taught her.

# DITCHES

## Verla Klaessy

To a young girl growing up on a farm, a ditch was a wonderful place to explore. Expanding on both sides of the gravel road this "borrow pit" was used to raise the level of the road for better navigation in the winter. The windblown snow would pile up in ditches, leaving less snow on the higher roads unless the storm was a full blown blizzard.

Our ditch was filled with sweet grass, weeds with flower heads, a few small trees and numerous surprises. In the spring many asparagus spears appeared, and my mother eagerly snipped them for a delicious addition to a rather humdrum meal. This part of the original prairie was not spoiled by spraying with weed control or cutting down to the bare ground as is the present custom.

As the fresh grass appeared I was allowed to be at my mother's side as she herded the sheep up and down the ditches as they munched the succulent treat. Someday it would be my job to become the shepherdess keeping the sheep off the road, watching for the mail man and waving to the neighbors as they drove by, carefully observing animals and caretaker.

As the flowers appeared I would pick bouquets for my mother. She would put them in a drinking glass or small milk bottle and place them on our kitchen table.

Dandelions were abundant as were violets, phlox, and tiny daisy-like blossoms.

One day I discovered a treasure. I had crossed to the opposite side of the road and found the ditch was blooming with strawberry flowers and gorgeous red fruit. I ran home and found a small syrup pail and hurried back to the newly discovered treat without anyone knowing where I had gone. Eagerly I picked the delicious berries until the bucket in my small hands became more than half full. Happily I rushed into the kitchen with my addition to the noon meal, a big surprise with lots of love thrown in for my mother. I could not believe that I was being scolded when she discovered I had crossed the road and was taking the berries from the ditch that really belonged to our neighbors.

Immediately after, my mother rang up the telephone to the neighbor and explained how her child had been trespassing and taken strawberries that had not belonged to her. I was broken hearted as I had been so thrilled at doing such a grown-up surprise.

The neighbor was very kind. She said she was not even aware there were berries growing there. And she had a strawberry patch in her garden and I was welcome to pick all I wanted out of the ditch. Such a relief that I had not committed a crime in mother's eyes. However, the sparkle of the moment had been lost and I never enjoyed future pickings as much as that first discovery.

A small tree growing in the fence line produced purple berries the size of the end of my finger. It was a mulberry tree, probably planted by bird droppings in previous years. These berries came off the branches easily and had a sweet, rather bland taste. We also had a mulberry tree in our back yard, resulting in yearly pints of fruit and jam on the shelves in the basement.

My cousin who lived in town came to visit often, and I was always eager to show her all the attractions of farm life. The mulberry flowers had turned into attractive fruit, and the two of us went to enjoy its bounty. After we had eaten an abundant amount, the juice turned our hands, cheeks, and the fronts of our dresses a deep purple. As usual, my mother was aghast. She immediately had us change our clothes and used Clorox water to remove the stain from our hands and our clothes with a sound warning that we were to stay away from the mulberry trees especially while my cousin was visiting.

Once in a while there would be a flutter in the grass and we would spy a pheasant with a small brood of chicks. The hen was a pale brown and could hide quite easily. A rooster, however, might be flushed and the bright colors of its neck and tail were a beautiful sight. I did not understand why he might become the main course on the dinner table.

Baby rabbits in a nest would be a joy my dad shared with me. I was fascinated as they hopped around, munching clumps of clover always wary of sudden movement or noise. Dad loved to make up stories about them and the rabbit stories became my favorite.

Winter with inches of snow building up in the ditches made wonderful sculptures in the drifts that formed from the wind blowing against the boundary fences. Our farm was flat land without a bit of hill anywhere. So the small mounds made in the ditch were great places for sledding. They usually sloped enough to make a short ride a delight. The visual reminded me of waves of water on the lake in summer. Being cold and wet from playing in the snow did not prevent me from going out again another day.

The ditches became fearful places the first year I walked the quarter mile to and from the country school. In late October, weird noises came from the ditches as I passed by after school. Without warning, an older boy or maybe two or three would hide in the tall grass and jump out to scare me, so I was crying all the way home. Sometimes the teacher, being aware of these tricks, would send me home early before the others were ready to leave. One day they taunted me that witches were going to come and steal my new baby sister. Frightened, I ran as fast as my short legs would carry me. I tried to jump over a low fence as I had seen the older ones accomplish. However, I did not quite make it. My lunch box flew open and a spoon flew out, striking me in the eye as I rushed to my mother's side in the house. I had a black eye for several days. And the boys were "requested" to stay after school until I had time to get home each day.

As I grew older and had a sister for a playmate it was fun for me to share all the exciting things I knew were in the ditches. Often our dog Trixie followed along sniffing here and there, chasing rabbits and just being our companion. Small adventures for small children, but growing up experience for facing our futures. The preparation for courage, taking risks, venturing into the unknown of climbing mountains or canoeing in a wilderness stream starts with a walk in the ditch.

**Verla Klaessy**, a great grandmother, spent her childhood on a farm during the depression years of the 1930s. She recalls vivid memories of the happy years spent with her sister and her parents.

# ANGELS ON THE HIGHWAY

## Richard Johnson

Our folks took my siblings and me everywhere when we were kids. We traveled to Iowa, Missouri, Arkansas, northern Minnesota, North Dakota and Wisconsin. Mostly we took summer vacations in the scenic Black Hills of South Dakota.

One year we reached eastern Wyoming. Very nice. But my eyes were locked on the distant Rockies. Our next-door neighbor, Bill, would return from Montana vacations with colorful tales of grizzly bears, bighorn sheep, and horseback trips to the high country. I was entranced. Knew I'd get there someday.

Years later, as a college student in the early 1980s, I hitch-hiked home the seventy-five miles from La Crosse, Wisconsin to Rochester, Minnesota. Not exactly a Big Sky Adventure, but it was something new. And it felt so good, so absolutely right, to stand out there and put my thumb out on that sunny autumn day. I was twenty-two and giddy with freedom. My first big solo adventure.

Ah, innocence. Ah, naiveté.

Got my first ride almost immediately. The happy-go-lucky young driver offered me a beer from his trusty cooler. I declined. He dropped me off near La Crescent, Minnesota, and I walked toward Winona.

And walked.

And walked.

And walked.

No one was into picking up hitch-hikers. The impetuous venture began to seem impossible. I felt vulnerable. Jeez. Would I end up sleeping in someone's barn? Or out in a field? This could be a bad deal.

I persisted, stubborn, even as those conflicting feelings increased. A carload of nuns zoomed past. The sisters averted their eyes. I probably would have done the same. I could be a dangerous criminal. You never know.

Finally, a car pulled over. *Ohdearsweetjesus. Another ride!*

The driver took me a good ways toward Winona before stopping at a tavern along Highway 61. "If you're still out here when I come out," he said, "maybe I'll pick you up again."

I was, and he did. Which is how I got to Winona. Where the troubles began.

I was tiring. Was considering buying a ticket at the Jefferson Lines bus depot when a multi-colored, renovated former school bus pulled up. Its boisterous young occupants promised they'd take me to Rochester.

I got in, ignoring my gut feeling.

Sure enough, the bus roared past the turnoff for Highway 14 and Rochester. I pointed this out to the driver. He jerked his head at a refrigerator wedged behind the first row of seats. "Shut up," he said, "and get me a beer."

"We're gonna make this as good for you as it is for us," one of the driver's friends said, ominously.

Great, I thought. These idiots are going to do what they want with me, and someday hunters will find a shredded backpack, a tennis shoe, and my mangled skeletal remains. Dental records will prove it was me. Huh. So *that's* what happened to Johnson . . .

"Just drop me off here," I said as we sped north on 61. To my relief, the driver did so. Kind of. He slowed the bus down to about 5 mph and made me jump out. The hard landing was worth it.

Anything, I thought, to lose these nitwits.

The drunks had me angry and agitated. Re-energized. So I made good time pounding the two miles back to Highway 14. What was left of it. Out in the country, past St. Mary's College (now St. Mary's University of Minnesota) and the College of St. Teresa (now Winona Cotter High School), there was only a reddish dirt trail.

Highway workers were preparing to repave 14. Not today, of course, but soonish. I was forty-six miles from home, staring morosely at an empty track where the doggone road should have been. Holy heck. Another fine pickle you've gotten us into, Johnson.

Cue the sad blues trumpet: *Wah. Wah. Wahhhhh . . .*

That's when an angel drove up on a side road to check his rural mailbox. He saw me cussing my luck and contemplating eternity, among other things, and came over to see what was up. I told him my predicament. He said not to worry; he'd get me as close to home as he could.

I climbed into his car and he cheerfully took me, via rustic backroads, as far as Eyota, thirteen miles from Rochester, where Highway 14 was still paved.

Thank you and God bless you eternally, kind sir.

It was getting dark. I was exhausted. Had one last desperate gambit. Called my folks from a noisy tavern in Eyota. Their phone rang just as they were leaving to go dancing, but I heard the sweetest words ever: "We'll come get you."

God bless Mom and Dad, the angels back home.

The least I could do was accompany them to the Eagles Lodge. Actually, I've always secretly liked polka music. And that night it never sounded better.


**Richard Johnson** is a freelance writer living in Mason City, Iowa. He loves to travel—finally made it to Montana!—but officially retired from hitch-hiking after that long, fateful day.

# MAJOR MISHAPS

### Marie Wells

In a family with six children there are likely to be a number of major mishaps. During the late nineteen twenties, we had our share of them.

Our family lived on a farm near Dickens, Iowa, in a house with no electricity or running water. Our weekly baths took place in the kitchen in those days. Mother would fill a large enameled basin with warm water from the reservoir at the far end of the ancient kitchen stove and set it on top of the stove to keep it warm. Since that range was the only source of heat in winter, she would carry in an upright kerosene heater as a supplement. The heater, made of metal, was about three feet high and a foot in diameter. The top had round holes in it to release more heat.

One Saturday night when I was three-and-a-half years old, mother undressed me and stood me on a kitchen chair between the heater and the range. When she went into the adjoining bedroom for a moment to get a washcloth, I lost my balance and fell on that scorching hot heater with my bare little bottom before tumbling, shrieking onto the floor. Mother frantically rushed back from the bedroom and gathered me up in a blanket while Dad dashed outside to start the car. We had a fast trip to Dickens to Dr. Bruce's office where he applied a soothing salve and bandaged my poor burned behind. Most of the skin was gone. It took weeks to heal. Mother felt so terrible! I can recall her holding me over my potty chair while we both had tears like tiny rivulets streaming down our faces. At three years old, I found out that life wasn't always kind.

We had to make our own fun on the farm. After our chores were finished in the summer, we would play outdoors in the grove, in the barn with our kittens, ride our red pony or play ball in the yard. Even these activities could lead to mishaps.

In August of 1929, when Dale was eight years old, he was riding Pet, our pony, into the house yard when he was brushed off by the gate post and broke his arm. A trip to Dr. Bruce's office resulted in a large cast on it. A few weeks later, Dad and my oldest brother, Howard, were sawing down and trimming dead trees in the grove for wood for winter warmth. They had just finished an enormous one about three feet in diameter, when Dale and Glen decided to walk the length of the fallen log from opposite ends. When they met in the middle and tried to pass each other, Dale who was much heavier bumped Glen who fell and received a compound fracture of his left arm. Panic ensued when the bone protruded from his forearm. Dad called to Howard to get the car. He picked Glen up and held him while Howard raced them to Spencer, to the office of an older doctor, who was also a surgeon. Dad believed that Glen would need surgery. It was nearly closing time and the doctor was in a foul mood.

Without giving Glen any anesthetic, he grabbed his arm with his huge hands, pulled and twisted the bone back into place, shouting, "Hold still, you little devil!" while Glen screamed.

He finally secured the bone, stitched the wound and applied a cast. Dad said later that he would have liked to have knocked that doctor flat. That would have been quite a sight since the doctor was six feet tall and Dad was less than five foot six.

In September of that year, Orville started country school for the first time. Two of the eighth grade boys thought it would be fun to play catch with him. As they tossed him back and forth, one of them dropped him. And of course, the fall broke his arm! So one more cast was applied to a Taylor boy. When the family attended the Clay County Fair, visitors who saw three brothers in casts, must have thought they came from a very abusive home.

That fall Dad bought a console radio enclosed in a large cardboard box. We were very excited about the new programs we would hear. After it was unpacked, I immediately adopted the box to play in with my kittens. A few days later, I was with my parents when they drove home from grocery shopping in Dickens. My brother and sister were already home from school. To my horror my brother Dale was cutting up *my box* with his pocket knife.

"That's my box!" I yelled, and thrust my foot next to the box just as Dale yanked down his knife cutting through my shoe and into my foot.

While Mother staunched the blood spurting from my wound, Dad rushed us the mile and a half back into town where Dr. Bruce neatly sewed up the cut. Dr. Bruce must have been very grateful for the amount of income the Taylor family provided.

When Glen was six he had the worst mishap of any of us. Howard had a spring loaded air rifle. Usually he was very careful to put it away. But one afternoon after squirrel hunting, he left it in the back porch. Glen, who was curious as a cat, picked it up and pretended to shoot it. He then turned it around and looked down the barrel. At that very instant the spring flew out and struck him in the right eye. He was in terrible pain. My parents hastened to take him to Dr. Bruce and to an optometrist in Spencer.

After his examination, his recommendation was to see a specialist. My parents hurried to telephone for appointments, first the clinic in Iowa City then to Rochester, Minnesota to the Mayo Clinic. The ophthalmologist at the Mayo Clinic told my parents he could not do anything to cure Glen's eye. He said there might be a cure in the future but there was none at the present. That incident resulted in Glen losing his eyesight in that eye for the rest of his life.

During the following years, we had numerous minor mishaps which were patched up with iodine and strips from clean worn sheets. We four must have learned to be more cautious from our previous experiences because we had no more major mishaps after the age of eight. I'm sure that was a great relief for our parents.

**Marie Wells** is retired after teaching school in northwest Iowa for thirty-four years. She enjoys church activities, attending plays, reading, writing, and visiting with friends, children and grandchildren.

# THE NUNS OF SAINT MARY'S

### Neal Keizer

When I was in fifth grade, my parents decided to enroll me at a nearby Catholic grade school. That we were Presbyterians didn't seem to matter to them, but it made me the odd man out. I had two older brothers, both in their teens, who'd been in their share of trouble recently. My parents hoped the strict routines and rigid discipline associated with a parochial school would keep me firmly on the law-abiding path.

It worked. I was so shell-shocked by the many differences between my old grade school and the new, that all my energy went to trying to fit in and get used to the heavier workload.

Sister Constance taught fifth grade. Back then the nuns wore the traditional black habit. Sister's head was encased in a starched white wimple covered by a black veil. Not a bit of hair showed, if she even had any. At her waist was a wooden rosary that reached nearly to her hem, the beads of which clicked softly whenever she moved. I thought she must be about eighty. But her wizened, homely face belied a gentle nature, and when she smiled, as she often did, she was transformed. I couldn't have asked for a better introduction to a new way of life.

The kids in my class, however, weren't so sympathetic. I was assigned to a desk in the third aisle, sixth row back. Directly in front of me sat a boy named Francis, who could fart silently, the odor wafting back to me with nauseating regularity. Behind me was Louis, who flicked spit-balls at the back of my head.

"Neal, why are you here instead of outside on such a beautiful day?" Sister Constance asked in my third week at St. Mary's, when she found me sitting alone in a corner of the library.

I could only shrug. To say anything would to be labeled a tattletale, which no boy wanted.

Sister took me by the hand and guided me from the library to the playground. She took me to the basketball court, situated on one side of the playground. A couple of nuns stood nearby, keeping an eye on the dozens of children on the playground. Sister Constance picked up a basketball from the blacktop at the base of the pole and tossed it to one of them.

Sister Agnes, a nun so young and pretty that I couldn't help but wonder why she'd chosen such a life, caught it, spun around, jumped and made a perfect basket! The other one, Sister Selma, scooped it up, dribbled it around Sister Agnes, and also made aim for the hoop. She missed, the ball bounced off the rim, but she leapt into the air and caught it, tried again and the second time the ball went through.

Before I knew it, I had joined their casual game, and not long after that a few more kids had come over to get in on the fun. I dodged and weaved with the best of them, making the occasional basket and earning praise from Sister Agnes. "Good shot, Neal!" she cheered, clapping her hands together after the ball I'd thrown circled the edge of the hoop at least four times before it finally fell through. I blushed and developed a huge crush.

A couple of weeks later Sister Constance recommended me for a job in the school kitchen. There I worked under Sisters Theodora and Monique, both short and round and prone to the giggles. I started out washing dishes. My pay was free lunch, which pleased my parents. Francis the Farter also worked in the kitchen, collecting trays and scraping the leftover food into the garbage before he sent the dirty dishes my way. He turned out to be not so bad after all, once we got to know each other.

The library was run by Sister Eugenia, who demanded silence and kept a ruler tucked in her sleeve. She could whip it out, grab a hand of the chatterer and render five or six quick slaps on the palm in quick succession. Much more painful than it sounds, and there were few repeat offenders.

I attended St. Mary's through fifth and sixth grades, before moving on to junior high. For the next fifteen years I continued to receive birthday cards from Sister Constance. When she passed away I attended her funeral, where Francis, Louis and I sat with a few of the many others who had been touched by her kindness over the years.

Author **Neal Keizer** went to a parochial grade school in Colorado, which he survived with minimal scarring and a deep, lasting respect for those who dedicate their lives to the calling.

# AN HONEST BOOK

## Brenda Wilson Wooley

A whole new world threw open its doors to me when I learned to read, and I galloped through those doors, arms open wide, devouring the written word like the country ham, red-eye gravy, and homemade biscuits Mother served for breakfast on frosty mornings.

I was six years old when I read my first book, *Pinafores and Pantalets*. After reading it dozens of times, I went on to *Heidi*, *The Secret Garden*, *Anne of Green Gables* and *Nancy Drew*, to name a few. When I grew tired of those books I read newspapers and women's magazines. Even the encyclopedia, when there was nothing else around.

Everyone in my family enjoyed reading, and our interests were varied. Mona, my mother's eighteen-year-old sister, read only romance magazines, and after each visit she left stacks of them behind.

"Can I read one of Mona's *Revealing Romances*?" I asked one day.

Mother shook her head.

"Why not?"

"You're too young."

"Why?"

"You just are."

After that I was always watching. And waiting.

My chance came a few days later. My mother was reading one of Mona's magazines and I was reading from the encyclopedia, our dog, Lucky, curled up beside me. I don't remember what came up, but Mother left the room. I sat for a moment, making sure she didn't come back, then I grabbed the magazine and darted out the door, Lucky trotting along behind.

For a few seconds I stood on the front porch, racking my brain for a place to read. When my gaze landed on the swing in our front yard, I knew I'd found the perfect spot. I spent a great deal of time there, reading, drawing and writing in my five-year diary. No one would suspect a thing.

I plopped in the swing and opened the magazine: *Darlene resisted, but Robert swept her into his strong arms and rushed to the bedroom. "No, no," she cried, her fists pounding his hard, muscular chest. Finally, she fell limp in his arms and his lips found hers, carrying her away on wave after wave of passion in a sea of throbbing emotion.*

Finally, I had found it—the "unspoken" stuff no one talked about. At least no one in my family talked about it.

After that, my head was buried in Mona's magazines every chance I got. I read them while sitting in the swing until Mother came outside to work in her flowerbeds. Then Lucky and I headed to my bedroom. This was also an ideal place, for whenever Lucky heard someone approach he let out a soft bark, giving me just enough time to shove the magazine under the pillow and grab my diary.

As the summer wore on, though, I became annoyed with the stories. After much chest-pounding and fervent kissing, the characters got married and lived happily ever after. I already knew not everyone lived happily ever after. And what happened between all the kissing and the living happily ever after? After reading all of Mona's magazines I could lay my hands on, I still hadn't figured that one out.

I read many books during the next few years, my obsession growing and fading. It returned in full force, however, when I read *Gone with the Wind.* I focused in on the night Rhett Butler got rip-roaring drunk. Wild with desire and out of control, he grabbed a resisting Scarlett and carried her up the stairs, two at a time, to their bedroom. I read it again and again. But like Mona's magazines, the in-between part was left out, skipping to Scarlett in her bed the next morning, a naughty smile on her face.

I was eleven, so by then I had my suspicions.

But all of my previous reading turned out to be small potatoes compared to what I discovered when I was fifteen.

It was deep summer and the days were sweltering, the nights heavy with humidity. Fog shrouded the hollows, and frogs croaked all night from the swamps nearby. I listened to my radio constantly, wandering around the house, dreaming about boys and dancing around my bedroom to the soft croons of The Platters' "The Great Pretender," Elvis's "Don't Be Cruel," and Fats Domino's "Blueberry Hill," which stayed at the top of the charts that whole summer. My mood fluctuated from euphoria to deep melancholy at the drop of a hat. Like the fog, I was hanging, drifting, waiting for something to happen.

Mona had married and was living in Indianapolis by then, but she came for a visit that summer, leaving behind her usual stacks of romance magazines. I had long ago lost interest in them, but in sifting through the stacks one day I came across a book. It didn't appear all that interesting, but out of boredom I picked it up and began thumbing through it.

Then I snapped to attention, excitement coursing through my body. This book was not your usual run-of-the-mill romance novel. This one would require real secrecy. I could neither sit in the front-yard swing nor sequester myself in my bedroom, so I called Lucky and we sneaked outside, walked down the dirt road near our house, took a path off the road and found a place where no one would be able to sniff us out. The spot was near a big oak tree on Walter Long's property, just over the fence that separated our land from his.

So it was there in Walter's field that I read the book that had jerked me up, spun me around and smacked me in the face with the real facts of life. I learned about sex, rape, incest, abortion, adultery, repression, and lust, things that had never been discussed before in conservative America.

Even newspapers, at that time, never mentioned such things. Finally, I had found a book that left nothing to the imagination, a book that would become a significant milestone in literary history.

I later learned that Canada had declared the book indecent. Parts of Rhode Island, Indiana, and Nebraska did the same, stating it would corrupt young minds. In 1956 many sexual acts were illegal. Birth control was unreliable and difficult to come by. Abortion was illegal, leaving many a woman to bleed to death in the back rooms of makeshift clinics or be branded for life by a judgmental society if choosing to have her baby and raise it on her own.

Not long ago, while ambling about in the public library, I came across a copy of the book that had so captured my attention. The minute I opened it I was swept back to that summer, experiencing it all again: the heavy, humid nights, fog shrouding the hollows, night frogs croaking from the swamps, the soft croons of "Blueberry Hill" drifting from my radio. And I was in Walter's field again, reading a book that refused to wrap everything up and tie it with a pretty bow. It was an honest book; one that would open the door to the feminist movement and change the literary world forever.

The book was Grace Metalious's *Peyton Place*, and this time I desperately wanted at least some citizens of that small New England town to live happily ever after. But few did.

**Brenda Wooley's** work has appeared in more than forty-five publications, including *The Birmingham Arts Journal, Kentucky Monthly Magazine, Barely South Review* and *Looking Back* magazine. She makes her home in Paducah, Kentucky, where she's working on a novel and a collection of short stories.

Photo provided by Joyce Jenkins

# LASTING FRIENDSHIPS

### Joyce Jenkins

I was a fourteen year-old farm girl, on the shy side, and it was difficult for me to make friends. My cousin Leota and I grew up together. She was outgoing and through her I became friends with her neighbors; Dolores, Doris, and Marcella. Later we became acquainted with two newcomers, Florien and Darlene.

In high school, our casual friendship developed into a bonding relationship that lasted into adulthood. Our personalities were different but our backgrounds and our values were similar. Darlene was daring and full of spunk. She treated everyone with kindness and respect. Dolores, Marcella, Florien, Leota, Doris, and I were the followers. At Christmas time we all got together and exchanged gifts; we gave ourselves the title, "We Seven."

Imagination was the starting point of our entertainment, and with Darlene, there were no limits. One spring evening when Darlene's parents were out of town, she came up with the bright idea that we should take her dad's car out for a spin. I had just gotten my driver's license and was skeptical of driving a strange car, but Darlene convinced me that no one would know the difference if we put the car back in the same place.

We took back roads so no one would see us. All went well until we went across a railroad track and the car stalled. We heard a train whistle and saw a train coming closer and closer. They all panicked and screamed, "Get it going."

I kept stepping on the starter and the car slowly jerked across the track just before the train came to the crossing. The screaming became silence and we sat there wondering, "Did this really happen?" To this day, each time I go across that track, I shiver and think what could have been.

We were fortunate to be alive. We knew we'd made a bad decision and rushed to get the car back exactly as we had found it. After several attempts, we were confident that no one could tell it had been moved. That was, until the next day when Darlene's dad confronted her. A neighbor had been watching us and tattled. Knowing Darlene's dad, we knew what the consequences would be, especially for her!

In desperation, Darlene decided to skip school, run away and go to her Grandma's in Eastern Iowa. She talked Leota into going with her. Between the two of them, they had a sack of jelly beans and a little money which they took from Darlene's sister's piggy bank. They left at noon and thumbed their way down the highway. With luck, they caught rides, telling fictitious stories that kept the drivers from being suspicious.

They spent the night sleeping in a haystack, covered up with hay to stay warm. The next morning they caught a ride in the back of a farmer's pickup. They eyed a sack of groceries and spied some bananas. By this time they were hungry and couldn't resist the temptation.

The farmer was headed in a different direction so he stopped and let them off. Little did they know their next ride would be in the back of a police car. The farmer with the pickup suspected they were runaways and contacted the police. They were surprised when the police car pulled up and they were told to get in. They were held at the police station until Darlene's dad arrived. Both girls were grounded for a month and had to stay after school for two weeks to write an essay the principal had assigned them for punishment.

Graduation was approaching and we realized the good times and school days were coming to an end, and that we would soon be parting our ways. We made a pact that we would stay in contact.

Darlene suggested we get together for one last time and go to a movie in our prom dresses. We were ushered down the aisle single file with Marcella in the lead right in front of me. Suddenly there was a chain reaction when all came to a halt. I didn't realize I was stepping on Marcella's dress.

She kept saying, "You're on my dress!" We were the center of attention for the entire theatre.

After graduation, Florien left to become a nurse and Marcella to become a cosmetologist, while the rest of us stayed in Hartley, working at various jobs.

In 1941, Dolores, Doris, and I went to California to work in a defense plant and Darlene moved to Texas with her family, leaving Leota behind.

Marcella was married in 1942. She and her husband joined us in California and Leota went to the east coast to marry her fiancée from Sanborn. By 1946 we were all married and all our spouses had served in the military

After the war, Marcella, Dolores. Florien, Leota and I returned to Hartley, where we made our homes and started our families. Doris and her husband moved to Ohio and we lost track of her. From that day on we were the "We Six."

A few years later Marcella and her family moved to Arizona and Florien and family moved to Colorado, but we stayed in touch. Throughout the years, Florien, Marcella, Darlene and their husbands would come back to Hartley to visit friends and family; we always got together for a good time, filled with fun and laughter.

It wasn't until class reunions and the Hartley Centennial that we were all reunited after 40 years. It was the first time since 1941. There was a lot of catching up to do. Darlene's husband played host and furnished food and drink. Being from the South, his southern accent and hospitality kept the party alive. Our big backyard made an ideal place for a party. Friends and classmates from high school joined us, which made the event enjoyable for all.

With passing years, our friendship became more and more meaningful. Age and health problems were taking a toll and we were concerned for one another. In December of 1998, we got word that Florien had passed away suddenly at the age of seventy-five. In 2002 it was Dolores at seventy-eight, in 2006 Leota at eighty-three, in 2008 Marcella, age eighty-five. I also learned that Doris had been living in Wisconsin and passed away in 2008 at age eighty-six.

Darlene's health was failing and she was confined to her home. We communicated regularly by phone. She was persistent in wanting me to come to see her. I decided to make the trip to Texas. We were both elated at being together again. We spent our time reminiscing about the old days and remembering the ones we lost. When we said our goodbyes, we were both aware that it was for the last time. A year later in 2010, I lost my last friend from the group. I have a special place in my heart for each of my dear friends and cherish their memories.

**Joyce Jenkins** resides in Hartley, Iowa, and started writing in 2010. Her stories are inspired by special memories of family, friends, and the times of her life that have brought many accomplishments. She enjoys the time she spends volunteering at the local nursing home.

# MY LIFE IN THE MOVIES

## Danny K. Marcotte

One of my earliest memories is of being in the darkened interior of a movie theater. About three at the time, I was too young to get anything out of the movie, but I liked being curled up on the cushioned seat, covered with the small crocheted blanket my mother had brought for just this purpose. Mom sat on one side of me, my grandmother on the other. When I asked about it years later, I was told that the movie had been *The Heiress* with Olivia de Havilland and Montgomery Clift, and I did vaguely remember a homely woman with severely dark hair on the screen. Many decades later I would see Carol Burnett spoof this movie, her impersonation of the bashful spinster character being dead-on and hilarious.

Widowed in the last days of WWII, my mother, only twenty-two at the time and six months pregnant, moved back in with her mother. They were both big movie buffs, rarely missing an afternoon matinee at the Palace Theatre in Waverly, Iowa. I'd even been named after one of Mom's favorite actors of the time, and the flickering of the silver screen was my lullaby. *Bedtime for Bonzo*, starring a future president of the United States, and *The Long, Long Trailer* were a couple of early favorites.

My first date, when I was thirteen, was with a girl named Eleanor Newman. We saw *Vertigo*, directed by Hitchcock. I loved the movie, my date said it made no sense and hated it, bringing to a quick end that particular romance.

When *The Music Man* premiered, the Palace Theatre was packed. Everyone was eager to see this movie about small town Iowa. And even though most everyone liked it, our high school band took to playing "Seventy-Six Trombones" until I wanted to pull my sweater over my head and scream. My mother, who had married again about that time, thought her new husband looked a lot like Robert Preston, though in my opinion it was more like Don Knotts.

Drive-in theaters were all the rage by the time I had my driver's license. My buddies and I watched *A Hard Day's Night* at the AutoVue Drive-In on the east side of town, sitting on the hood of my stepfather's big Chrysler and swatting mosquitoes. We also saw *The Birds*, another Hitchcock favorite, and *Son of Flubber* there, but when the drive-in closed for the winter we were again driven indoors. Some movies were never shown at the drive-in, for fear of what passing motorists might accidentally glimpse. During the winter months we glutted ourselves on *Lolita, Sex and the Single Girl* and *Goldfinger*, considered racy at the time but mild by today's standards.

I met my wife at a movie theater. She was working behind the ticket window at the Englert Theatre in Iowa City, where I was in my senior year of college. When I purchased a ticket to see *Wait Until Dark* she told me it was a terrific movie. The dazzling smile she gave me, combined with her shoulder length strawberry blonde hair, reminded me of Ann-Margret in *Bye-Bye Birdie.*

She was right about the movie, but even though it was one of the most suspenseful I'd ever seen I couldn't give it my full attention. My mind kept wandering back to the girl with the pretty smile. Afterwards, when I saw she was just finishing her shift, I hung around and struck up a conversation.

Allison and I dated for three years, going to countless movies, taking turns in deciding what we'd see. When she sat gamely through *Where Eagles Dare*, a WWII action film, I knew she was the girl for me. My proposal was carefully planned. A movie, of course, followed by a walk through the park, where I would get down on bended knee and take out the ring I'd bought. The movie I chose for this momentous occasion was *Love Story*. It sounded perfect. I didn't know Ali MacGraw was going to die at the end!

We emerged from the theater with Allison sobbing. I nonetheless stuck to my plan. She continued to sniffle and blow her nose as we walked. When I finally took out the ring to pop the question her eyes were puffy and her nose red, but to me she was beautiful. She accepted,

Like Bogie and Bacall, we were meant to be together. So it seemed only natural that for our honeymoon a year later, we'd go to Key Largo.

For years **Danny Kaye Marcotte**, not wanting to get beat up in school, never let anyone know what his full middle name was. He eventually came to appreciate his mother's sense of whimsy. A kidney-transplant recipient, he has retired and moved to Florida with Allison, still the girl of his dreams.

# VITAMEATAVEGAMIN

## Alyce Redmond

We got our first television set when I was about five years old. My older brother Walt brought it home one day, after trading his scooter for it. The owner of the funny-looking little box had regretted the purchase, saying it would never catch on. Dad, a tinkerer like my brother, was immediately fascinated, and set the television up on the coffee table, replacing the bowl of fruit that had been there. He and Walt adjusted the metal poles on top of the box, which they explained were called "rabbit ears" and would help us get a clear picture.

At first I didn't find any of the shows my parents watched very interesting. They liked something called *The Texaco Star Theatre*—it was really spelled that way—and *The Pulitzer Prize Playhouse*, which was especially boring! Walt's favorite show was *You Bet Your Life*, a game show with a funny-looking guy called Groucho Marx. I didn't for a minute believe that was his real name and I failed to understand why my family would stop what they were doing to watch these shows when there were other more interesting things to do. Like playing paper dolls with me.

Then something happened. A new show appeared on the airwaves. Starring a goofy redhead and her husband with a Cuban accent, *I Love Lucy* was an immediate hit throughout the country. I joined my family in the living room to watch each episode. We laughed as Lucy took ballet lessons and got her foot stuck on the practicing bar; when she became convinced that the new neighbors were plotting a murder; and when she and Ethel accidentally bought too much beef and put the wrapped packages in a baby carriage to sell at the local butcher shop. In that same episode Lucy was accidentally locked in the walk-in freezer. When her icicle-encrusted face appeared at the freezer window my first reaction was to gasp in horror. To my young mind it was too frightening, too real, and for the next few days I swore I wouldn't watch the show again.

By the time it came around for the next episode, however, I'd recovered, and sat in my usual spot on the floor in front of the sofa, with my father's legs on one side of me and my mother's on the other. I was soon glad I'd relented. It was the best episode ever, the one where Lucy gets an opportunity to be on a TV commercial. The product she was demonstrating was called Vitameatavegamin, which, unbeknownst to Lucy, contained twenty-three percent alcohol. With each take she became funnier...and we, in our living room, grew increasingly hysterical.

"Are you unpoopular?" Lucy asked, slurring her words and leaning on the counter she was standing behind.

Even Mom, a strict teetotaler, couldn't help but laugh. When the episode was over we continued to talk about it, rehashing the funniest moments. In trying to describe his favorite part, Walt stumbled over the difficult word, making a mash of it.

"Vitameatavegamin," I said, getting the name of the elixir exactly right.

Dad tried, but did even worse than Walt had. Mom just threw up her hands in defeat.

"Vitameatavegamin!" I yelled. Then, to everyone's amazement, I began the commercial pitch, word for word. "Hello friends, I'm your Vitameatavegamin girl. Are you tired, rundown, listless?"

Walt laughed, slapping his thighs.

Encouraged, I continued. "Do you poop out at parties?"

Somehow I remembered the entire thing perfectly. I had my family in stitches, which, of course, made me feel like the star of my own show.

For the next few days I repeated the commercial at least a dozen times. When my mother's friends stopped by for afternoon coffee, she encouraged me to "Do Lucy for us." I did, and their praise was so lavish that I puffed up with a sense of importance. I stopped by Dad's shop and wowed the guys there. Even Walt's friends, who'd come over to work on his new scooter, were impressed. For a while, anyway.

Eventually the glow began to fade. When the Avon lady stopped by and I started in, Mom cut me off and told me to go outside and play. Walt kicked me out of the garage, and even Dad was losing patience. I got the hint. By the time the next episode of *I Love Lucy* rolled around, we were all ready to move on.

Decades later, Lucy endures, the show just as funny today as it was back then. And every once in a while, at a holiday or family gathering, someone will ask me to do the Vitameatavegamin commercial. I still remember it, word for word.

**Alyce Redmond** is a retired teacher. She started out teaching middle school, eventually becoming vice-principal. She has been married and widowed twice, and now spends much of her time as a volunteer at one of the most respected hospitals in Madison, Wisconsin.

# LAW AND DISORDER

## Mark Smith

The story you are about to read is true. The names have been changed to protect those who have since become respectable.

The date: April 1, 1975.

The place: Mason City, Iowa.

April 1st fell during spring break and our gang couldn't let this opportunity go to waste. We were known as the R.O.L. (Royal Order of Lumberjacks) after a Monty Python sketch. So far our pranks had been limited to pie attacks and some creative use of toilet paper. In an earlier event two of us had visited our psychology teacher, Mr. Anastaia, at his home. In the course of the visit Quinn asked to use the restroom. Once inside he opened the restroom window and passed Mr. A's toilet paper out the window to waiting hands who then used it to decorate his trees and lawn. We came back the next day to clean it up, but hey, we'd TP'd him with his own toilet paper! Even our rivals the FRNIRG (Friday Night Rowdy Group) had to admit that was pretty cool.

That's the way it was in '75. Nobody got hurt, nothing got broken, and everybody had fun. But the April 1st of our senior year called for something special, and boy, were we ready.

The morning started at Marty Quinn's house. Marty's home was our meeting place, where we watched Monty

Python and planned hijinks. With our connections to the school's drama club and scrounging abilities, we had put together a reasonable facsimile of a WWI doughboy uniform, right down to the flat helmet and puttees. As I dressed myself we went over the plan a final time.

At the heart of Mason City's downtown district stands the Cerro Gordo County Courthouse. Just outside the front door is a statue of a WWI soldier. With a rifle in one hand and a grenade in the other, he stands a tribute to those who served in "The War to end All Wars."

As Dan Hammers, our driver, pulled up to the curb I slid out of the back seat and put on the helmet. Retrieving a bolt action shot gun from the trunk—the statue had a bolt action rifle and we wanted to look authentic—I made sure that the gun was empty and the bolt was open so people would know the gun was empty.

Dan vanished and Marty followed me as I stormed into the reception area. "I QUIT!" I hollered. "It's cold out there. It's lonely, I don't get any veterans benefits—AND LOOK AT WHAT THE PIGEONS HAVE DONE TO MY HELMET!"

The receptionist sat at her desk, staring at me in shock and people were coming out from the adjoining offices to see what all the commotion was about. It was time for my big finish. "Get somebody from World War Two to stand on that pedestal. I'M LEAVING!" and I marched out the door singing *Mademoiselle from Armentieres*.

As I *hinky-dinky parlez vous*-ed myself out the door Marty leaned across the reception desk and said *sotto voce*, "April Fool," then sprinted for the door.

The poor lady finally found her voice. "Was this a joke?" she cried. "Were those two together? What is going on here?"

As we ran to the car parked outside, two things surprised us. First, Dan was not with us. Second, and more important to the person standing on the main drag dressed as a WWI solder and carrying a gun, Dan had locked the car doors.

Marty ran around the side of the court house, supposedly to find Dan but nevertheless removing himself from pursuit. Unable to flee, I duplicated the statue's pose and hoped for the best. Time passed s-l-o-w-l-y.

Marty and Dan ran back to the car a few minutes later. "Why aren't you in the car?" Dan yelled.

"You locked it"

"Oh." He reached past me and opened the door. "Stop wasting time and get in!"

I probably should have reminded Dan not to end his sentence with a preposition, but instead chose to toss the gun into the trunk and the helmet into the backseat, then throw myself in after it. Then we were off to wreak more mischief.

That afternoon our April 1st grand finale was planned. I would be driving in my car, the "Nader Hater," a 1964 Corvair that left a trail of oil everywhere it went. As an added bonus the heater wouldn't turn off and it filled with smoke from the fore-mentioned oil leak. Dan refused to ride in it, saying he was afraid of being gassed, but I drove it everywhere.

This time I would be driving to the back door of the police station.

The plan was simple. Three of us were going to reenact the great Dillinger bank robbery, *our* way.

I parked the Corvair behind the police station. We got out of the car and shoved our way through the back door. Six of Mason City's finest were standing around the desk. All motion stopped as they turned around to see three teenagers dressed in trench coats and slouch hats stumble through the back door. We were holding red plastic dart pistols and a baby blue toy machine gun.

"This isn't the bank!" we shouted. We performed a perfect Stooge withdrawal with the three of us simultaneously cramming ourselves through the doorway and out to the parking lot. We'd piled into the car and hit the street before the police could even react.

Laughing all the way, we drove back to Marty's place. We were proud of our stunning victory, planning bigger and better mischief for the rest of spring break.

That night Jill, Marty's girlfriend, was at work at the movie theater. She was running the concession stand when

Officer Red Murphy stopped by to get a cup of coffee. Taking a sip of his coffee, he spoke casually. "A bunch of kids busted into the station today, pulling some silly stunt. We were going to grab them and lock them up for a few hours and teach them a lesson, but they were too fast and got away."

"Um . . . that's too bad," Jill stuttered.

Officer Murphy looked across his coffee cup, straight at Jill. "If they try anything else, we'll get them."

The Royal Order of Lumberjacks did not meet again for a month.


**Mark Smith** grew up in rural Iowa, in a family of seven. His formative years were filled with adventures involving animals (wild and domestic), snow, firearms, the odd explosion or two, and way too much work. He insists that he has flashbacks as a result of his upbringing. His family chooses to refer to them as "daydreams." He has been published in several anthologies, a national magazine, and is the author of *Storm*, a children's book.

# THE SECOND VISIT AT CHRISTMAS

## Tom Phillips

Recently I traveled back to the homestead, long since abandoned and now crumbling and desolate on the prairie. It was a true pioneer's claim, miles from the nearest neighbors and tens of miles from the nearest town.

My mother was born and grew up in that place; in a home whose final appearance gave it a special flavor. At a time when most of the early farm houses were small, one or two-story frame rectangles, not much more than functional shelters, hers had a character all its own. Small wings of rooms extended past the central core of kitchen, pantry, dining room and parlor, giving the structure almost a letter "H" configuration.

There had never been a plan to make it that shape. At least that's what the members of her generation claimed. It just happened that way. As each new child came along, a tiny room was added. By the time there were nine children, two miniature but graceful wings lent stature to what had originally been—like all of the others—a one-story rectangle.

The house must have always been under construction—and always busy. To supplement the family's income, my grandfather carried the mail in a horse and buggy to the surrounding farms and communities with names that have now receded into the distant past: Star, Venus, Dorsey, Red Bird. Each was a small cluster of dreamers whose creameries, blacksmith shops, and sawmills have long since vanished.

My grandfather's mail deliveries kept him away from dawn until dusk, so from an early age the children tended the garden, milked the cows, carried corn cobs to the house to start the fires, and dumped the ashes from them when the embers had cooled.

To earn enough to go to teacher's college, my mother worked for three years at a country store in Walnut, Nebraska. Walnut is gone now, too, but even in its heyday it was only a single building that housed a post office and a general store with groceries, seeds, hardware, and assorted small tools and dry goods.

When she had saved enough money, my mother used it to get her teaching certificate at Wayne State Teacher's College, and for several years she taught all eight grades at a nearby country school. Hanging on a wall in my house is a teaching contract we found in the attic when her house was sold. It is for the school year beginning 1 September 1930, and my mother was to be paid $675 for the year. There is a penned-in note on the contract written by a school board member that states: "Teacher agrees to start her own fires."

She must have been a very good teacher. Fifty years later, she was still getting letters from her country school students.

It was the visit to the homestead and all the other recollections that reminded me of my mother's story about the special event that was part of her Christmases there.

In her family Santa Claus came twice, first on Christmas Eve and then again with a single gift on the evening of New Year's Day. My mother did not know what prompted her parents to celebrate in that fashion and neither she nor I have heard of that tradition in other families. Perhaps they conceived of it as a way to get the New Year off to a warm and positive start, or maybe they were just trying to put a lid on the rambunctiousness of nine very active children and make the long Midwestern winter seem a little shorter. Or, they may have seen it as a reward for the hard work the children had to do to help run the farm and share in each other's care.

Quite possibly, it was a combination of all those things.

I suspect though, given my mother's example, that sharing and responsibility were important reasons. In recent years I've come to wonder if there was another essential ingredient as well. The *timing* of Santa's second visit—New Year's Day—has always intrigued me. Was it intended as one more small illustration that no matter what happened in the lives of the children over the next year, they would always be cherished by the people inside that home? That whatever events befell them, they would always find warmth and love there . . . Santa would *always* return, just for them, on New Year's Day?

It's easy to over-analyze an idea that may have simply bubbled up from the hearts of two caring parents. Clearly though, it was a signal to the children that they were loved in a special way. Surely the example must have been obvious to the nine of them. Even one small extra gift from Santa's second visit could not have been easy for the family to manage during difficult times. It was a lesson about the true value of things, taught in a gentle and marvelous way.

In my mind, I picture my mother as a young girl inside that house, bright with the excitement that must have occurred when Santa made his second, special, visit on New Year's Day. She would have waited for him in the glow of the fire from the Franklin stove, toasty warm near the firebox, a little cooler at the edges of the room. Just the family, cherishing one another, in the small house set in a snowy and frozen landscape in the midst of an immense horizon.

**Tom Phillips** grew up on a farm near Lincoln, Nebraska. After thirty-six years in the military, during which he led a unit through a terrorist episode, served in Operation Desert Storm, and led some of the first American troops into Sarajevo, he worked as a university administrator before beginning a full-time career writing about Americana, military and defense issues, and baseball.

# PIESTENGEL

## Brad Gray

Growing up in New England with its abundance of Cortlands and Macintoshes every fall, I spent some time, as did my Yankee forebears, experimenting with ways to make hard apple cider. But it was not until I went to Iowa that I learned the country method of home winemaking.

In the spring of my senior year in college, I applied to the University of Iowa for a graduate program in English, and was accepted. Some months later, my wife and I found ourselves in Iowa City or, more accurately, living in a small house in Oxford, Iowa (pop. 705) because we couldn't find any place to live closer to the university.

I learned many interesting and useful things during my three years at the university: that the possessive form of Charles Dickens' name can be spelled either "Dickens'," or "Dickens's," but never "Dicken's;" that a spondaic foot in English poetry consists of two stressed syllables that neither rise nor fall; and that an elegiac quatrain is a four-line stanza, rhymed or unrhymed, in iambic pentameter. But the most useful thing I learned in Iowa, by far, was how to make *piestengel*.

It came about in this wise.

My neighbor in Oxford drove truck for a local livestock-hauling company, but he was essentially a man of the soil. Every spring he planted a large vegetable garden out back of his house and he also worked his grandmother's small farm out near Swisher, raising soybeans and corn. I think my neighbor considered me somewhat odd since, in his view, I knew nothing about country living and always seemed to have my nose stuck in a volume of John Keats' odes, but he tolerated me, and we became friendly.

One day, in the late spring of the year, he invited me out to his grandmother's farm to show me around. I turned off the paved road at the RR1 mailbox, drove down a dirt road past rows of corn, and arrived at a house that looked quite a bit like the house in Grant Wood's painting, *American Gothic*, except without the Gothic window. The first thing I noticed was a dozen very large hills of rhubarb growing out by the old run-down barn. Actually, this was the second thing I noticed. The first was the carcass of one of their guinea hens that had flown up to the power transformer, electrocuted itself, and was still up there.

"What do you do with all of this rhubarb?" I asked.

"Make *piestengel* out of it, mostly," said my neighbor.

"*Piestengel?*"

"Yeah, rhubarb wine," he said. "Some folks don't like it that much but I'll tell you one thing; it'll straighten out your day." And he proceeded to tell me how he made it.

I found out later that *piestengel* was one of the original German wines produced in the Amana Colonies, just down the road from Oxford. Rhubarb, or "pie plant" as my grandmother used to call it, is usually thought of as good for pie filling and not much else. But for the locals in this rural part of southeastern Iowa, many of whom are of German descent, the best use of rhubarb is for making *piestengel* ("*stengel*" is the German word for "stalk"), a somewhat tart white wine with a slightly pinkish tint.

Probably brought over from the Old Country, their recipe for making rhubarb wine relies on natural fermentation and is simplicity itself. For example, rather than adding cultured yeasts, yeast nutrients, anti-oxidants and other commercial ingredients, the natural or wild yeast on the fruit is allowed to do the fermentation work. The yeast breaks the sugar in the juice down into alcohol and $CO_2$. The $CO_2$ is given off as a byproduct, producing a bubbling or boiling effect (the word "ferment" comes from the Latin *fermentāre*, "to cause to rise or boil"). When the yeast has converted all of the sugar to alcohol, it dies and falls to the bottom of the container (for my purposes, a plastic milk jug) as sediment. The remaining alcohol content by volume (ABV) is about 10-12%.

With the recipe for making the wine in my head, and with several large armloads of rhubarb my neighbor had insisted on piling, leaves and all, in the back of my old Toyota station wagon, I drove back to Oxford and went at it like a professional *Weinhändler* (vintner): cut the stalks into one-inch pieces and mash with a 2 x 4, add the boiling water and the sugar, stir with a wooden spoon, strain through cheese cloth, pour into clean plastic milk jugs, wait eight weeks, and finally, "rack" the wine to clarify it (i.e., siphon it off into another container leaving the sediment in the first container).

The months passed after this initial foray into the winemaking business and soon Thanksgiving had again rolled around. And again, my neighbor and his family invited my wife and me to Thanksgiving dinner, just as they had the year before. Only this year I was able to contribute to the feast by bringing along a couple of bottles of six-month-old wine that I had labeled, Old Swisher Farm Piestengel.

It was hard to tell with my neighbor sometimes, but I think he was pleased.

**Brad Grey** received his M.A. degree in English from the University of Iowa before embarking on a career in book publishing as an in-house acquisitions editor. Currently a freelance editor and writer, and an avid outdoors enthusiast, his articles have appeared in *Bird Watcher's Digest* and *Common Ground*, a local land conservation newsletter. He lives in Massachusetts with his wife, Virginia, and a large Newfoundland dog, Siegfried.

Photo provided by Karen Howard

# THE ICE SKATES

## Karen Howard

The Kinney Shoe Store in Waterloo, Iowa occupied a store front on East Fourth Street, across from the upscale, five-story Black's Department Store. The shoe store had two big display windows flanking the entry, each holding the latest 1950s shoe fashions.

While I waited for the city bus to arrive and take me on the half-hour trip to Evansdale, where I lived, I would scour the display of shoes. And there, in the far corner along with those awful zip-up women's goulashes trimmed in fake fur that chafed your legs above the ankles with raw, red circles, was a pair of white figure-skates.

I was an eleven-year-old girl who longed to possess them. As soon as I spotted those skates, they called my name and I knew I had to have them. My allowance and babysitting money combined would not stretch far enough to make the purchase. Desperate to buy the skates and the fun they promised, I made a bargain with my parents. Dad and Mom would pay half of the price of the ice skates and I would cover the balance. The rest of the bargain was that the ice skates would be my Christmas gift—and they would be my only Christmas gift. The Santa Claus that visited our house was on a nearly nonexistent budget, and I had three other sisters who were expecting Christmas gifts. The bargain was struck.

On Christmas morning, in the wee hours before my parents and sisters stirred, I crept out to the living room. Under our spindly and sparsely decorated Christmas tree were the beautiful white ice skates, with my name on them! And to my surprise, I had another gift—a pair of denim blue jeans with a front zipper. In those days girls were only allowed to wear dresses or skirts to school, but the teenagers on Disney's, *The Mouseketeers* wore jeans. I was ecstatic, and can honestly say it was my best Christmas ever!

I made pom-poms from leftover yarn for my skates, but could not afford to buy the rubber guards to protect the blades. Every afternoon after school I skated until dark, no matter how cold. Often I was in such a rush to get there that I would put my skates on at home and walk all wobbly the three blocks to the Triangle, a useless piece of land across from the Grace Baptist Church, at the curve where McCoy Road and Sixth Street intersected. The city flooded it each winter, creating a large span of rough ice for skating. The remainder of the year it was fallow and full of sandburs, but during the winter it was a magical place for me. I not only learned to ice skate, I also learned to skate backwards and do figure eights. I played crack-the-whip and occasionally skated with Marvin D. or Bob M. It was a heavenly place for a girl and the beginning of my boy-girl relationships.

The Triangle is now gone, as is the church and the homes of my girlhood friends. Interstate 380 came through Evansdale about thirty years ago, removing all of those landmarks. Though the landmarks no longer exist, they remain vivid in my memory.

Those white ice skates still hang in my garage. The leather is cracked and the blades are dull with rust. I am no longer eleven years old and I no longer ice skate, but those dingy white and rusted skates remain among my most prized possessions. No matter my age, when I see them hanging there I'm transported back to the Triangle, flying along on the ice, laughing with my friends, carefree and young again.

**Karen Howard** lives in Hartley, Iowa, with Rose, her golden retriever. She enjoys her family, reading, writing, and quilting—but working in her yard, not so much.

# PURPLE AND PINK BABY CHICKS

## Debra Sue Edwards

Easter was a big deal in our family. It was a time of family gathering, when relatives would take turns hosting an Easter Sunday feast that often outdid even the one at Thanksgiving.

My sister Jodie and I always got new dresses and shoes for the occasion, and we would receive straw Easter baskets brimming with marshmallow eggs, chocolate rabbits and assorted other treats nestled in beds of bright green plastic grass. We looked forward to it every year, even if Mom did limit us to one treat of our choice per day. At the time we resented this constraint—they were *our* baskets, after all. It was not until we were older that we understood.

Our family was hosting the Easter dinner the year I was eleven and Jodie was eight. Grandparents, aunts, uncles and cousins galore were due to descend on our house that day, coming from as near as across the street to as far away as Wisconsin. After Jodie and I had spent most of Saturday helping Mom clean the house and do some preliminary baking, we would be rewarded on Sunday morning with our Easter baskets.

Still in our pajamas, we rushed the kitchen, where Dad sat at the table with his cup of steaming coffee. Two baskets sat on the table in front of him. But there was something different about them. Instead of being encased in transparent plastic, the baskets were open, and in among the fake grass and foil-wrapped candies, something moved.

Jodie and I both froze in our tracks. Then we heard it: a distinctive *cheep-cheep*. The green plastic rustled. Standing at the sink, Mom turned to watch us, a smile on her face.

The chicks had been dyed Easter colors for the holiday. Balls of fluff. Mine was pink and Jodie's was purple. We squealed with delight.

Holding mine in the palm of my hand, I said, "Your name is Bubblegum," and stroked the little creature gently.

Jodie, for some reason, named hers Hector.

We set Hector and Bubblegum in a cardboard box lined with old dishtowels, handfuls of brown grass and crumbled leaves we gathered from the backyard. Only when we were convinced they were comfortable did we put on our new Easter outfits.

When family began arriving and our cousins wanted to see the chicks, we hovered over them protectively, letting them look but not touch.

"They're just a couple of dumb chickens," sneered thirteen-year-old Randy.

I stuck my tongue out at him.

The chicks matured quickly. Within days the down had been replaced by pinfeathers, and their legs and necks grew longer. As their feathers came in, their colors began to fade. Within a couple of weeks Hector was no longer purple, but instead was covered with glossy brown feathers. Bubblegum, however, retained some of her pink. At the base of each tan feather was a hint of the previous color, most noticeable when she fluffed herself up.

Soon they moved from our bedroom to a pen in the back yard. During the day they were allowed to wander about in the fenced yard, where they scratched happily at the grass and dirt for bugs. Before long they looked like full grown chickens.

That's when the problem began. Maybe Jodie had suspected something after all, for Hector turned out to be a rooster. And he crowed. A lot. We lived within the city limits, where we were pretty sure farm animals weren't allowed. One day Dad said, "I talked to your Aunt Betsy. She says Hector and Bubblegum can come live at her place. You girls can go over there and visit as much as you want."

Our Aunt Betsy, a hard-working spinster, lived on a small farm not far from the outskirts of town. Her yard and pasture held a couple of ponies she let us ride when we visited, some geese, two pigmy goats and plenty of chickens. Her old rooster had recently died, so she was happy to have another. It was the perfect solution.

So our Easter chicks went there, and adjusted to their new home with ease. Mom and Dad took us to see them whenever we wanted. It wasn't long before Hector, king of the roost, no longer acknowledged us. Bubblegum, however, with her faintly pink-tinged quills, never failed to fluff up happily upon my arrival. Over the course of her first year her unique hue gradually faded, but by the time it was gone I was able to spot her anywhere, color or no.

Hector lived to be nearly nine years old. Then one morning Aunt Betsy noticed he wasn't crowing, and found him lying lifeless in the yard. A senior in high school, Jodie had more pressing concerns on her mind, and just said, "Oh, okay. Thanks," when our aunt called to give her the news.

Three years later my chick was also gone. One of the ponies had wandered through an open gate and stepped on her. By then I had married, moved out of state and was expecting my first child, but I cried when I got the news. I hadn't forgotten our colorful Easter chicks. I hadn't forgotten Bubblegum.

**Debra Sue Stueven Edwards** lived most of her life in Highland, Indiana, moved to Chicago after her marriage and then back to Indiana when she was widowed at the age of thirty-two. She has three children, now grown, who encourage her writing and hope she will someday pen her memoir so they can learn more about the father they hardly knew.

# WHEN TRAINS CAME TO TOWN

## Carolyn Rohrbaugh

When I was growing up in the 1940s and '50s, passenger and freight trains rumbled each day into Sutherland. A passenger train, affectionately called a "puddle jumper," made a round trip every day from Eagle Grove to Hawarden, Iowa, carrying passengers and mail to the towns along the way.

Men who hooked rides on freight trains and begged to trade work for food or money were referred to as hobos or bums. The most familiar hobo was Hungry George. He was tall and thin and carried his belongings in a gunny sack slung over his shoulder. Some parents told their children if they were naughty Hungry George would put them in his sack and carry them away, but those who knew him said he was a kind man and a talented musician who could tune a piano better than anyone. His pay for this task was usually a hardy meal. We didn't have a piano, but Mother was always happy to share our garden vegetables with him. We were also told that he carried a diamond in a tobacco can and was willing to show it to anyone who asked.

Hungry George rode the train from town to town for a few years, then disappeared. No one knew what happened to him, but some people speculated he might have shown his diamond to an unscrupulous person and met a tragic end.

I was fascinated with the trains and loved hearing their whistles blow as they rounded the curve into town. One day Mother announced we would ride the train to Paullina, ten miles away, to visit our relatives. I imagined we would be traveling in one of the freight cars with the hobos, but Mother told me she had purchased tickets and we would ride on the passenger train.

My only memory of that trip was when I had to go to the bathroom. We had an outdoor toilet at home so I didn't expect much, but upon entering the train's rustic toilet I peered through the hole in the wooden toilet seat and saw the ground passing beneath. I ran out of there as fast as I could, afraid I would fall through the hole and be run over by the train.

When we were a little older, my sister Darla, our friends Patty and Mike, and I played along the railroad tracks. Coal lined the tracks so we were usually pretty dirty by the end of the day. The railroad linemen rode on a motorized hand car to check the tracks. A steady "putt, putt, putt" warned us when they were returning and we scampered away as they yelled at us to get away from the tracks or a train would run over us.

One day, feeling particularly rebellious, we took a penny we'd found and laid it on the tracks. Mike told us it would wreck the train. When we heard the blowing of the whistle we ran to the tracks to watch the train derail, but it just rumbled over the penny with no ill effects except for leaving a very flat penny. Deep inside I was relieved to see that we hadn't caused such a catastrophe.

Passenger trains to Sutherland were discontinued long before I was grown, but freight trains continued to carry grain and cattle to and from town for several years.

On September 10, 1980, the Chicago and Northwestern engine #4602, made its last trip through Sutherland. Soon after that the railroad tore out the tracks and trestles.

**Carolyn Rohrbaugh** has lived in Sutherland, Iowa, her entire life. She has been involved in the community, including on the city council and as mayor. She is retired and spends her time writing, gardening, and with her family.

Sketch by LaVonne M. Hansen

# FARM SALE ON THE HOME PLACE

## Marilyn Kratz

For most of us on the Northern Plains, the blustery winds of March signal a coming change in seasons. But, for retiring farmers years ago, those winds blew in a major change in life style. March was, probably still is, the traditional month for farm sales, although we don't hear much about them these days.

A generation or so ago, many retiring farmers handed their land over to a son or daughter, moved to a nearby town, and continued to assist with farm tasks. But more recently, the younger generation has been lured away by careers in cities often hundreds of miles from "the home place."

Such was the case, on March 4, 1995, when my uncle Elton Thum, now deceased, contemplated retiring from the southeastern South Dakota farm which his parents had worked before him. When a cousin made an offer for the place, Elton and his wife Charlotte accepted it, wondering how that decision would affect the lifestyle they'd known throughout their married life.

Elton and Charlotte set a date early in March and began the tasks familiar to many retired farmers now residing in small towns across the plains.

As he worked, Elton remembered good years with abundant harvests and bad years when everything seemed to go wrong. He knew he wouldn't miss the frustration of hurried trips to town during busy harvest times to buy replacement parts for his well-used machinery. But he still felt a special affection for his tractor, the only one he'd ever purchased new.

Charlotte made decisions about which household items to sell and which ones to move into their new home in a nearby town. Each item brought back memories of years working together with her husband to raise a family and build a successful life.

A few days before the sale, Elton arranged the machinery in rows in the yard. Boxes of small household items and farm tools were set out on flatbeds. They would be sold before the larger items.

Gray skies threatened snow as the crowd gathered on sale day. After household items were sold, many women retreated into the warm farmhouse kitchen. As they visited over coffee and sweets furnished by neighbors and relatives, Charlotte could hear echoes of all the laughter she'd heard over the years in that cozy room.

Outside, men warmed themselves with coffee and sandwiches bought at a lunch stand set up in the yard for the day. They moved from one machine or tool to the next, indicating their purchases by barely perceptive nods as the auctioneer rattled off numbers at a dizzying pace.

The usually friendly farm dog curled up in a corner beside the house steps and watched the proceedings with a somber look in his eyes. The Thums regretted they would not be able to take him into town with them. They felt relieved when another farm couple offered to take him. The dog climbed willingly into his new owner's pickup. He seemed eager to escape the changes around him.

Heavy snow fell as the last items were sold late in the cold afternoon. Soon darkness hid the unfamiliar look of the empty farmyard. The family gathered in the kitchen to assess the day, relieved to have it end.

A week later, Elton and Charlotte Thum drove away from their old home for the last time. Ninety years of ownership by two generations of the same family had ended. A new home waited for them. It would seem strange at first, but they'd get used to it. They knew they could drive by their old farm every once in a while in years to come, just to keep in touch with it, because, to Elton and Charlotte and their extended family, that farm would always be "the home place."

(Previously published in *The Fence Post*, Ogallala, Nebraska, and *The Observer*, Yankton, South Dakota, both weekly publications.)

**Marilyn Kratz** is a retired elementary teacher and freelance writer from Yankton, South Dakota. She has had five books and more than 600 magazine stories, articles, and poems published. She writes a nostalgia column for a Yankton weekly and is a regular contributor to *Living Here*, a regional magazine published in Yankton. Her newest book, *Feed Sack Dresses and Wild Plum Jam - Remembering Farm Life in the 1950s*, is a collection of articles, poems, photographs, and recipes relating to growing up on a farm and is available on Amazon.com.

# THE SUMMER ATTIC PROJECT
## A True Midwest Story

### Marilyn C. Ford

The Empire Builder train waited at the small North Dakota station as my family and friends stood waving to me. It would soon be taking me to college, fifteen hundred miles from home. I was nineteen and felt like an orphan as I boarded the train destined to head west, from the open prairie to the Pacific Ocean.

My mother's parting words were, "Remember, we'll clean the attic in the spring."

The train whistle blew as I boarded it. A few tears mixed with my almost-brave smile as the train pulled away from the familiar.

The conductor took my bag. "Your ticket, Miss. Your seat is next to the window and you can wave to your folks again." It felt like a huge kindness, and I thanked him.

I sat looking out the window as the fall season moved into the western mountains toward Puget Sound, where I would live for the next nine months. I'd be studying, but also waiting for spring and summer and Mom's chicken and biscuits with gravy. Home and the promised attic project waited.

When spring finally arrived, I boarded the train that would take me back to Cando, North Dakota. I had promises to keep.

My mother and Dad met me at Devils Lake, Mom in her kitchen dress and Dad in his field clothes. They were grinning as they hugged me. I wasn't an orphan. I was home.

The attic room faced west, with two large windows that absorbed the heat of the afternoon sun. The two windows had long ago been painted shut in the one hundred and two year old house. The single hanging bulb with a brass pull chain provided extra light. Air movement was felt only by the buzz of the flies trying to escape the heat. It was arm-pit dripping hot and I didn't have an escape plan.

I had made a promise. Now it was time to wrap my hair in a red bandana and get to work. Three generations of stored history were in this room, along with blown field dirt that had found places to settle and appear as a part of the décor.

With the determination of a coal miner on his first day on the job, I got to work. I could do this! My tools were simple: boxes, broom and wastebasket, labels, marking pens, dust mask and surgical gloves. What I hadn't planned for was my mother being the Chief Executive Officer, hereafter called CEO, but she was a lot of fun and knew her attic history.

The CEO sat on her vanity-bench, making suggestions, giving history to each item, where to put them or to whom they should be given. This was going to take awhile and we both knew it. Much longer than the couple of months I would be home.

One particularly hot day, after we were dripping and dirty, she had an idea. "Let's call the girls on the block and have a coffee party!"

Brilliant! The work stopped. I called "the girls" while the CEO cleaned up. I took frozen cookies from the freezer, set out napkins, cups and sugar. After a shower, fresh clothes and a swipe of lipstick, I was ready. Time for the magic show! The audience of seventy and eighty-year-old ladies brought a sense of renewed life to the old house.

CEO Mom told everyone about our attic project. I noticed she didn't mention the many antiques we'd uncovered. There were some serious collectors in this group of women. I poured coffee and listened.

Summer was passing and the project was progressing very slowly, but we took time out for coffee and tea at the oak table, surrounded by laughter that brought light to faces of the women. They recalled their own days past, their daughters, the churning of butter, carrying barn lanterns to find their way safely home during a dirt or snow storm.

"Please pass the coffee and another cookie, if you don't mind?" More laughter. No one was in a hurry to leave.

The summers passed, and changes were happening. The attic continued to reveal its surprises. The coffee get-togethers continued, with "What did you find today?" becoming the traditional response when the phone call was received.

"Come and see the best find ever," Mom or I would reply.

My mother, now in her wheelchair and wearing a bright smock dress, held the great find of the day, a doll with porcelain face, real hair, cloth arms and legs and tiny leather shoes, its blue lace dress covering a pretty slip and cotton bloomers.

Cries of "Oh, oh, oh, can I hold her?" filled the room.

"Of course," Mother always said, even though this was her only doll and it was beautiful.

Five summers later the attic at last had a defined shape, with walls. A previously hidden closet held more treasures that would be given to the Hawk, Rugby, Egland and Cando Museums.

Then, one summer day, Mother said, "I'm sorry I'll miss out on your final fun with the attic project."

It had kept her going, but she knew she wouldn't see it to the end. Mother died at age eighty-two, exemplifying how to live life and how to pass on with grace.

After examining the attic room after her funeral, I gently closed the door on the late summer light that filtered through the west window. It was summer in North Dakota.

Mother was right about missing out on the fun. Perhaps she was watching, and I hoped so. It took another four years, three baby boys, two college degrees and three home moves before I returned to do the final sweep of field dust from the attic. The day I finished I called the daughters of the original coffee group to come for coffee and cookies.

I had a few treasures to show them.

**Marilyn C. Ford**, a graduate of Cando, North Dakota High School, is the author of the "The Hired Man," a short story in the anthology *Amber Waves of Grain*. She studied poetry and writing under the guidance of Ted Luciani, and regularly shares her stories at churches and clubs. She continues to write, watercolor and take classes.

Photo provided by Chris Devaney

# TRIBUTE TO A SALESMAN

### Susan Dunn Schmid

My brothers, sisters and I adored school. That our Irish-German parents were sharecroppers and resources were few, certainly had something to do with that. And while we kids were plenty bright, mischievous and enterprising, left to ourselves for too long we'd eventually hit dry dock. School was a sure-fire cure for our boredom.

The place we called home was a tired, wood-frame farmhouse perched atop a hill at the end of an obscure, half-mile dirt lane. Neither our house nor the farm place it anchored were visible to passers-by on the connecting gravel road. When late May heralded the last day of school, my siblings and I always felt a big letdown, for summer too often meant isolation and what seemed imprisonment. By June's end, our fears were realized as fields of Iowa grain surrounded and all but swallowed us up. That old lane was so poorly maintained that few outsiders acknowledged it, let alone ventured onto it. And with plenty of chores to do and bean fields to walk, we rarely traversed it ourselves.

So, wasn't it heaven when our confinement would occasionally be interrupted by the adventurous farm-to-farm salesman who'd negotiate our rutted lane, pull into our yard in a cloud of dust and find himself quickly surrounded by five wide-eyed urchins looking upon him like Lazarus risen from the dead!

The Fuller Brush Man, the Watkins Man, the Hoover Vacuum Cleaner Man, the Schwan's Ice Cream Man were just some of our summer-time saviors.

It was an itinerant merchant of encyclopedias, however, who ultimately transformed our lives, selling our parents a set of children's encyclopedia called *The Book of Knowledge* (copyright 1953). I don't know how our parents could have ever afforded them, but what a gift they were! Thrills and wonders—including "Things to Make and Do"—waited inside each volume.

The literature and poetry selections, enhanced with enchanting graphics, were my particular favorites and were cherished companions during subsequent summer days or inclement weather. I adored the rhythm, meter, and rhyme of poetry and would spend hours reading and re-reading nursery rhymes and classical poems. To my second grade class in Greenville, Iowa, I delivered my first recitation from one of these books, "The Old Woman and Her Pig" *(Anonymous)*. I liked how the words rolled off my tongue and made music. I was delighted when my peers seemed to like the story, too.

As years passed and we kids left home, this beloved and well-worn set got left behind or destroyed. How my heart ached to have lost the source of so much joy! When my children were born, I searched to find as many of these nursery rhymes, poems and stories as possible and read them aloud to my darlings, hoping to pass on this love for good literature.

Divine providence confirmed that this passion should be fostered for another generation when, after my husband and I moved to Texas in 1989, we happened upon an identical set in pristine condition at a flea market in Austin! I screamed with delight when I saw them all lined up as though they were waiting just for me.

Now my very own set of *The Book of Knowledge* rests proudly on the bookshelves of our home, waiting to be read to our grandchildren. Perhaps these cherished volumes will help inspire at least one to become a prolific reader, writer or poet.

Still today as I dust, and stop to open one of these treasures, I'm carried back to those sweet summer days of youth when these pages befriended me and opened my eyes, mind and heart to a large and fascinating world beyond those fields of grain. And I pause to thank my parents, now long gone, and that brave salesman who ventured up a rutted dirt lane to rescue the likes of me.

**Susan Dunn Schmid** is retired from a career in corporate America and now delights in the 4G's: God, Gardening, Grandchildren and Gratitude for it all! After her childhood and young-adult years in Iowa and Minnesota, she and her German-native husband, Max, call central Texas home. They return to Iowa and Minnesota regularly to nurture relationships and celebrate the bounty and blessings of the beloved Midwest.

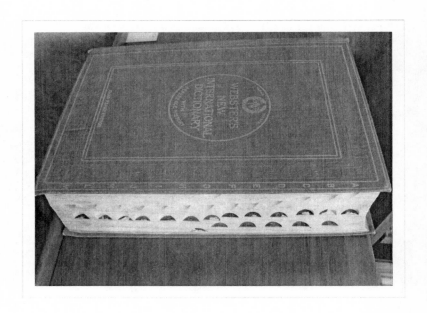

# READING, WRITING, AND THE PEANUTS GANG

## Jean Tennant

Math was never my strong subject, so when I first entered Mr. Trepanier's classroom many years ago, I went with the usual low expectations and a chip the size of a blackboard eraser on my shoulder. The desks at the back of the room beckoned, and I found one that allowed me to slouch down low while I chewed on the end of a pencil and scribbled bits of angst-filled prose into a spiral notebook. Writing was my way of dealing with the turmoil that came from being a gloomy fourteen-year-old, the byproduct of an unhappy home life.

Then, one day, Mr. Trepanier approached my desk. Head down, I didn't see him coming.

"Snoopy is an aspiring writer," he said, speaking so softly that no one else heard. He gave no lecture about paying attention in class, not even a suggestion to put the notebook away. Just that comment, given because he'd noticed I was always writing. I sat up in my seat and feigned interest for the remainder of the hour.

It didn't take long to figure out that Mr. Trepanier was crazy about Snoopy, Lucy and the whole *Peanuts* gang. He brought the subject up often during class, and we'd enjoy a few minutes' respite from the usual dry instructions to talk about Schroeder and his piano, or Pigpen and his accompanying cloud of dust. A daily fix from the newspaper wasn't enough for Mr. Trepanier. He bought

157

paperback copies of the *Peanuts* comics and claimed to have every one of them. I never doubted it.

Although I continued to write in my notebook, I did less of it in that class than I might have, and almost against my will I began to catch on to some of the complexities of mathematics. My grades slowly improved. Not much at first, but enough to offer some encouragement.

I learned that fractions with common denominators are called "like fractions," and that Linus sometimes used his security blanket as a formidable weapon.

I started asking Mr. Trepanier to explain some of the lessons to me, usually after the bell had rung and the other students were scurrying from the room. He always took the time to go over a lesson again, then would balance the tutorial with a snippet of information about the latest *Peanuts* cartoon or character. These moments of individual attention were enough to brighten the rest of my day.

Mr. Trepanier taught me how to divide positive and negative fractions, and lent me a book that showed Snoopy on top of his doghouse, pounding away at a typewriter. He asked me about my own writing, and I told him a little about my situation at home. He listened, passed no judgments, and showed me a *Peanuts* comic that featured Peppermint Patty, who lived in a single-parent household.

I learned how to calculate the perimeter and area of a figure, and when Mr. Trepanier told the class that *A Charlie Brown Christmas* was going to be on TV, I made it a point to watch. I loved the story of the unwanted little Christmas tree that became magnificent with care and attention.

"Thanks, Charlie Brown," I'd say as I left his classroom, my casual wave belying the impact this time had on me. In hindsight I should more accurately have called him Lucy. Lucy, the amateur psychiatrist with her "The Doctor is IN" sign and price tag of five cents per visit.

I began to read the *Peanuts* cartoons in the daily paper in the school library. My grades in math crept up, went from barely passing to acceptable. I still asked for help with things I didn't understand, but sometimes after class I stopped just to talk. I borrowed his paperbacks, returned them, and bought some of my own.

He encouraged my writing, told me to read everything I could get my hands on, and made suggestions. Soon I was devouring not only *Peanuts*, but the works of S. E. Hinton and whatever else I could find in the library. My own writing became less morbid, and I saw more humor—and hope—in the world around me.

I stopped sitting way in back, and I participated more in class discussions. I still didn't like math, but I liked Mr. Trepanier, so it seemed the polite thing to do. When I occasionally raised my hand in response to a question, Mr. Trepanier always called on me, and I'd sometimes spout "Good Grief!" instead of one of the less savory expressions that had previously peppered my vocabulary.

He was a part of my life for less than a year, this kind man with the quirky sense of humor and endless patience. Near the end of the second semester I told Mr. Trepanier that my family was moving—again. He listened, nodded, and said, "You'll be fine. The things that are important, you'll take with you."

What I took with me was a stack of paperback books, a better understanding of math, and a slightly brighter outlook on the world.

Thanks, Charlie Brown.


**Jean Tennant** started writing early, with her poem being published in *Highlights* magazine, the result of a grade school teacher's submitting it. Throughout the years teachers have held an important place in her life. She will be forever grateful to them for their encouragement, inspiration and, in the case of Betty Taylor, friendship.

## OTHER BOOKS BY SHAPATO PUBLISHING:

*Walking Beans Wasn't Something You Did With Your Dog: Stories of Growing Up in and Around Small Towns in the Midwest* (2008)

*Knee High by the Fourth of July: More Stories of Growing up in and Around Small Towns in the Midwest* (2009)

*Amber Waves of Grain: Third in the Series of Stories About Growing Up in and Around Small Towns in the Midwest* (2010)

*Make Hay While the Sun Shines: Fourth in the Series of Stories About Growing Up in and Around Small Towns in the Midwest* (2011)

*Sowing Wild Oats: Fifth in the Series of Stories About Growing Up in and Around Small Towns in the Midwest.* (2012)

*Horse Woman's Child: A Novel About Clashing Cultures on the American Frontier* by Roger Stoner (2011)

*The Earth Abides* by Betty Taylor (2010)

*Mama & Asha* by Carolyn Rohrbaugh (2012)

*The Callie Stories* by Karen Jones Schutt (2011)

*Marcia's Life Application Bible: A Living Translation* by Marcia Zubradt Cheevers (2012)

*Turning Around the Heart: Stories of Possibility, Connection, and Transformation* by Cindy Chicoine (2012)

*TheDirt: Family Life on an Iowa Farm— Stories to Entertain and Inspire* by Karen Schwaller

# SUBMIT YOUR STORY

The next Midwest anthology–no title yet–is due for publication in late 2014. If you'd like to submit a story for this or future anthologies, here are a few things to keep in mind:

- Send a true, original story of 600 – 1200 words.

- A Microsoft Word document as an email attachment is the preferred method, though submissions by mail–typed, please!—are also accepted.

- The deadline for each anthology is April 30th of the publication year.

- Photographs are welcome. A copy is preferred, but if you send an original it will be scanned and returned to you. Shapato Publishing accepts no responsibility for lost photographs, so be careful about sending those precious family photos.

- Payment for your story if accepted for publication is $10 upon signing of the contract, plus one free copy of the book when available.

Any of these details may change at any time. Nostalgia is always welcome, but so are contemporary stories if they fit in with the general theme of the anthologies, which is upbeat. Send to:

Email: jean@shapatopublishing.com

Mail:   Jean Tennant
       Shapato Publishing, LLC
       PO Box 476
       Everly, IA 51338

CPSIA information can be obtained at www.ICGtesting.com
Printed in the USA
BVOW05s0844151215

430328BV00004B/545/P